～本書を活用した大学入試対策～

☐ **志望校を決める（調べる・考える）**

入試日程，受験科目，出題範囲，レベルなどが決まるので，やるべきことが見えやすくなります。

☐ **「合格」までのスケジュールを決める**

基礎固め・苦手克服期 … 受験勉強スタート～入試の 6 か月前頃

・教科書レベルの問題を解けるようにします。

・苦手分野をなくしましょう。

→ 教科書レベルの長文がほぼ理解できている人は，
『**大学入試 ステップアップ 英語長文【標準】**』に取り組みましょう。

応用力養成期 … 入試の 6 か月前～ 3 か月前頃

・身につけた基礎を土台にして，入試レベルの問題に対応できる応用力を養成します。

・志望校の過去問を確認して，出題傾向，解答の形式などを把握しておきましょう。

・模試を積極的に活用しましょう。模試で課題などが見つかったら，『**大学入試 ステップアップ 英語長文【標準】**』で復習して，確実に解けるようにしておきましょう。

実戦力養成期 … 入試の 3 か月前頃～入試直前

・時間配分や解答の形式を踏まえ，できるだけ本番に近い状態で過去問に取り組みましょう。

志望校合格！！

長文読解のキーポイント

◎ **構文を見抜く**

英語の文の成り立ちを見抜き，しっかりと英文の意味をとらえるようにしましょう。

◎ **等位接続詞 and / or / but / ,（カンマ）に着目し，文の構造をきちんと把握する**

等位接続詞などが英文中にある場合は，その接続詞が何と何を結びつけているかを見極めて，英文全体の構造を把握できるようにしましょう。

◎ **省略されている語句をすばやく見抜く力を養う**

英文中には動詞など，一部語句が省略されている個所もあります。どの語句が省略されているかを推測し，英文の意味を捉えられるようにしましょう。

◎ **代名詞，代動詞が何を指しているのかを，きとんと理解する**

英文中で，代名詞や代動詞が使われている場合，どの名詞や動詞の代わりとして使われているかを注意深く読み解き，英文を正しく理解できるようにしましょう。

〜本書のしくみ〜

本冊

基本的には，見開き2ページで
1単元が完結する構成です。

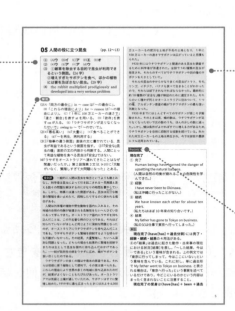

■notes

英文中の難しい単語・熟語には訳をつけています。語彙を増やすためにもしっかり確認しましょう。

☆重要な問題

大意把握など，ぜひ取り組んで，きっちりと理解し，内容をおさえておきたい問題です。

解答・解説

解答部分を赤く示し，解説との見分けをつきやすく工夫したので，単元単位でしっかり理解を深められます。

詳しい解説つきです。正誤確認だけでなく，解答するときのポイントになる解説も注目しましょう。

各問題に全文訳を付けています。
英文の意味が十分理解できなかったところは，適宜参照しましょう。
特に大意把握の問題の中には，全体の流れがわからないと解けない問題もありますので，全文訳を確認しましょう。

Point

長文に出てきた重要な文法事項を取り上げ，例文と和訳，解説を掲載しています。

📖 本書の活用例

◎ 実際の入試問題に取り組み，まとまった英文を読むことに慣れ，繰り返し読んでいくうちに，英文を早く，正確に読む訓練ができます。

目 次

本書に関する最新情報は，小社ホームページにある**本書の**「**サポート情報**」をご覧ください。(開設していない場合もございます。)
なお，この本の内容についての責任は小社にあり，内容に関するご質問は直接小社におよせください。

There was a skinny young boy who loved football with all his heart. Practice after practice, he eagerly gave everything he had. But being half the size of the other boys, he got absolutely nowhere. At all the games this hopeful athlete sat on the bench and hardly ever played. This teenager lived alone with his father. Even though the son was
5　always on the bench, his father was always in the stands cheering.

When the young man went to college, he decided to join the football team. Everyone was sure he could not be a member. But the coach (a)enrolled him because he always put his heart and soul into every practice, and （　A　） the same time, provided the other members （　B　） the spirit and hustle they badly needed.
10　It was the end of his senior football season, and as he ran onto the practice field shortly before the big playoff game, the coach met him with a telegram. The young man read the telegram and he became deathly silent. Swallowing hard, he (b)mumbled to the coach, "My father died this morning. Is it all right if I miss practice today?"

The coach put his arm gently around his shoulder and said, "Take the rest of the
15　week off. And don't even plan to come back for the game on Saturday."

Saturday arrived, and the game was not going well. In the third quarter, when the team was ten points behind, a silent young man quietly slipped （　C　） the empty locker room and put on his protector. As he ran onto the sidelines, the coach and his players were surprised to see their faithful team mate back so soon.
20　"Coach, please let me play. I've just got to play today," said the young man.

The coach pretended not to hear him. He didn't want his worst player in this close playoff game. But the young man persisted, and finally feeling sorry （　D　） the young man, the coach (c)gave in. "All right," he said. "You can go in."

(d)Before long, the coach, the players and everyone in the stands could not believe their eyes.
25　This little unknown, who had never played before, was doing everything right. The opposing team could not stop him. He ran, passed, blocked, and tackled like a star. His team began to catch up. The score was soon tied. In the closing seconds of the game, the young man ran all the way for the winning touchdown. (e)The fans broke loose. His team mates carried him on their shoulders with joy.
30　After the stands had emptied and the team had showered and left the locker room, the coach noticed that this young man was sitting quietly in the corner all alone. The coach came to him and said, "I can't believe it. You were fantastic! Tell me what got into you? How did you do it?"

He looked at the coach, with tears in his eyes, and said, "Well, you knew my dad died, but did you know that he was blind?" The young man swallowed hard and forced a smile, "(f)Dad came to all my games, but today was the first time he could see me play, and I wanted to show him I could do it!" ³⁵

［白百合女子大］

(1) 空所（ A ）～（ D ）を埋めるのに最も適当な語を１つずつ選べ。（2点×4）

　　ア into　　イ under　　ウ for　　エ at　　オ with

(A)	(B)	(C)	(D)

(2) 下線部(a)～(d)とほぼ同じ意味になるものをそれぞれア～エの中から１つ選べ。（4点×4）

		ア	イ	ウ	エ
(a)	enrolled	registered	curled	encouraged	shouted at
(b)	mumbled	cried	said quietly	fumbled	begged
(c)	gave in	offered	rejected	ignored	compromised
(d)	before long	after a while	then	soon	long time ago

(a)	(b)	(c)	(d)

(3) 下線部(e)の意味に近いものをア～エの中から１つ選べ。（4点）

　　ア ファンは転げ落ちた。

　　イ ファンは喧嘩を始めた。

　　ウ ファンは狂喜乱舞した。

　　エ ファンは帰り始めた。

☆ (4) 下線部(f)を和訳せよ。（6点）

I feel like I'm losing my mind.　Over the last few years, I've had an uncomfortable feeling that someone, or something, has been changing the way my brain works.　I haven't completely lost my mind, but I can feel it's changing.　I feel it most strongly when I'm reading.　I used to find it easy to get lost in a book or a long article.　That's
5　rarely the case anymore.　Now my concentration starts to drift after a page or two.　I read a little bit, then start looking for something else to do.　I feel like I'm always pulling my lazy brain back to the text.

I think I know what's going on.　For well over a decade now, I've been spending a lot of time online, searching and surfing the Internet.　I'm a writer, so the Internet
10　saves me a lot of time doing research.　I use my computer to pay bills, schedule appointments, book flights and hotel rooms, and many other tasks.　Even when I'm not working, I'm reading and writing emails, scanning headlines, flicking through Instagram, watching short videos on YouTube, or just jumping from link to link.

These are all advantages, both for work and play.　Such easy access to information!
15　But these advantages (a)come at price.　The Internet is not only a channel of information.　It also shapes our thought processes.　And what the Internet seems to be doing is reducing my ability to concentrate and think.　(b)Whether I'm online or not, my mind now expects to take in information the way the Internet sends it to me: in a fast-moving stream of tiny information packets.　My calm, focused mind is being pushed
20　aside by a new kind of mind that wants to take in information in short, unrelated, and overlapping bursts —— the faster the better.

Some time ago, a research company published a study of the effects of the Internet use on young people.　The company interviewed 6,000 kids who have grown up using the Internet.　They reported that the Internet has affected the way the young people
25　absorb information.　"They don't necessarily read a page from left to right and from top to bottom.　They might instead skip around, scanning for important information of interest."

We humans used to have a 'linear' mind —— a mind that was good at processing long, difficult text, without losing concentration.　But now, that's changing.　For the last five
30　centuries, ever since the printing press made book reading a popular activity, the linear mind has been the center of art, science, and society.　Now, that mind may be a thing of the past.

[北星学園大-改]

(1) 各問いの答えとして最も適切なものを，それぞれア〜エの中から1つずつ選べ。(6点×5)

① Why does the author find his mind wandering when reading long text?

ア He has become used to browsing information on the Internet.

イ He likes YouTube too much.

ウ He has stress because of doing research with kids.

エ He has many tasks to do, such as paying bills and booking travel.

② What does the author mean by "come at a price" in the underlined part (a)?

ア Paying for an Internet connection is expensive.

イ The price of books has increased since the days of the printing press.

ウ The Internet is costing us our ability to think deeply.

エ The Internet costs us time due to distracting content.

③ What was the main finding from the research of young people?

ア Young people's process of taking in information has been affected.

イ The company interviewed six thousand children.

ウ Young people can't read very well because of the Internet.

エ Companies are trying hard to understand the effect of the Internet.

④ According to the text, which of the following best describes a 'linear' mind?

ア The ability to use traditional printing technology.

イ The ability to read a variety of text from art, science, and society.

ウ The ability to read text from left to right.

エ The ability to keep focused on long and difficult text.

⑤ What does the author think about the Internet?

ア He is happy he can take in information faster now.

イ He thinks the benefits, such as easier research, are greater than the costs.

ウ It is robbing us of something important and special.

エ With time, we will be able to concentrate better.

☆ (2) 下線部(b)を和訳せよ。(5点)

■ notes

4. get lost in ～「～に夢中になる」　5. drift「あてもなく漂う」　11. book「～を予約する」

12. scan「～をざっと読む」　headline「(記事などの)見出し」　flick「ざっと見る」

19. packet「パケット，転送単位に区切られたデータのまとまり」　push aside「～を脇へ追いやる」

21. overlap「重なり合う」　25. absorb「～を取り入れる」　26. skip around「飛ばし読みする」

28. linear「リニアな，線で表される」

When I was about ten, the highlight of the school year was a field trip to the Robert Chocolate Factory in Antananarivo, Madagascar. The memories of its large white rooms and store full of chocolate boxes came back to me yesterday, when my wife gave me a bar of chocolate from that same factory, now (A) sale in a famous

5　store in London. It's under a different brand, *Sambirano*, but a little research reveals that it's not only made by Robert, it is also the result of a fascinating movement called Equitrade.

Equitrade is related to Fairtrade, but it differs in some important ways. Fairtrade is ultimately about growers, and ensuring fair prices to small-scale farmers and

10　producers. A fair price for crops is guaranteed, but the goods themselves, and hence the profits, are made elsewhere. (a)Equitrade aims to support the sale of finished goods, rather than raw materials, with all the (①) value of a completed product. In this way, the majority of the profits stay within the developing economy, taxes are paid to the local government, and the whole country benefits from the trade.

15　To follow the example of the chocolate bar, the average Fairtrade chocolate bar costs about $2.20, according to John Vidal, a journalist for the British newspaper The Guardian. Only a tiny share of that sum stays in the country where the cocoa beans were grown, around two to three percent of the price you pay. Because the actual chocolate is made elsewhere, the rest goes to the developed world producers,

20　the supplier, the retailer, and so on. Because Equitrade works to keep the whole production chain local, 51% of the retail price of a bar of *Sambirano* stays in Madagascar. I'm sure you'll agree that this is considerably better.

There are a number of (②) related to Equitrade. The first is that there is a transfer of expertise to the developing country. In this case, entrepreneurs worked

25　with the UK's Academy of Culinary Arts, Britain's leading association of chefs and restaurant managers, to prepare their chocolate for the market. The Robert factory has been producing confectionery for the (③) market for decades, but now produces a world-class product that can compete internationally. That transfer of expertise runs all the way down through the chain to the farmers, who are using better methods and

30　growing better beans thanks (B) technical support from the UK.

Secondly, there's real prestige for Madagascar here. Connoisseurs have admired Madagascar's cocoa beans for a long time, and wider recognition of that is not a bad thing. That the *Sambirano* was not just grown but also processed and packaged in Madagascar should be a real source (C) pride for this poor country that shares

35　its name (D) a famous animated movie. Building the reputation of Madagascar internationally is great for national self-esteem, and also attracts further investment, and thus further development, jobs, and economic growth. Another important factor in Equitrade is tax. Because more money stays in Madagascar, the government gets a larger share, in this case 11% of the value of a chocolate bar. That is paid into the national treasury and makes education, healthcare and public spending projects 40 possible.

(注) expertise「専門知識」 entrepreneur「起業家」 confectionery「菓子類」 prestige「名声，威信」
    connoisseur「愛好家」 investment「投資」 national treasury「国庫」 　　　[立命館大-改]

(1) 空所（　A　）～（　D　）を埋めるのに最も適当な語を1つずつ選べ。同じものは2度は使えない。

(2点×4)

　　ア with　　イ to　　ウ for　　エ of　　オ against

(A) [　　　] (B) [　　　] (C) [　　　] (D) [　　　]

(2) 空所①～③を埋めるのに最も適当な語(句)を1つずつ選べ。(4点×3)

① 　ア mediocre　　イ face　　ウ low　　エ added
② 　ア rumors　　イ web sites　　ウ effects　　エ regulations
③ 　ア local　　イ high-end　　ウ fruit and vegetable　　エ international

① [　　　] ② [　　　] ③ [　　　]

☆ (3) 下線部(a)を和訳せよ。(6点)

[　　　　　　　　　　　　　　　　　　　　　　　　　　　　　　　　　　　　]

☆ (4) 本文の内容と一致するものを2つ選べ。(6点×2)

　ア Eleven percent of the chocolate produced in Madagascar is consumed locally.
　イ The author thinks Equitrade is much better than Fairtrade.
　ウ The chocolate factory that the author visited as a child was in London.
　エ The transfer of expertise was very helpful for the economy of Madagascar.

[　　|　　]

インド人の時間感覚

　　Indians seem to take no thought of time.　Seeing the Indians' way of life, I am inclined to wonder if they can understand the meaning of the proverb, "Time is money." Their lives seem to be moving slowly, unconscious of time.

　　I once went to the ticket counter of an airline company in New Delhi in order to buy
5　a ticket to Bombay.　Though people were waiting for their turn in several long lines, they seemed not to mind being kept waiting a long time.　In the meantime, (a)<u>the young female clerks were attending to their duties leisurely</u>, with their beautiful saris waving gracefully, regardless of the lines of people.　It took me nearly three hours to reserve just one ticket.　Soon after that, I found it was the same with the telegraph service at
10　the Telegraph and Telephone Corporation.　I wanted an Indian friend in Bombay to come and meet me at the airport, so I had a telegram sent to him.　But gazing at the clerk slowly attending to his business, I began to fear that it might not get to my friend during that day.

　　My fear came true!　I could not find my friend when I reached the Bombay airport
15　the next night.　Finally I managed to find my way to his place only to hear that the telegram had not yet been delivered.　(b)<u>I was puzzled that my friend didn't look surprised in the least.</u>　The telegram was delivered the next afternoon.　That is, two whole days after I had sent it.

　　From the viewpoint of the Japanese who are rushing all the time, Indian life seems
20　inconvenient, but it is very interesting to notice that they don't feel it is inconvenient at all.　We force our doings into the frame of time, always being chased by various engagements or businesses, while Indian life seems to go on leisurely with the slow passage of time.　What a big contrast on this same earth!

（注）sari「サリー」（民族衣装）　　　　　　　　　　　　　　　　　　　　　　　［駒沢大］

■ notes

1. *be* inclined to *do*「～したいと思う」　8. regardless of ～「～を気にせずに」
15. manage to *do*「何とか～する」　23. passage「経過」

☆ (1) 本文の内容に最もよく一致するものをア～エより１つ選び，記号で答えよ。(6点×5)

① ア Indians seem to be unaware of the passage of time.

イ Indians seem to trouble themselves with time.

ウ Indians seem to like the practical wisdom of time, "Time is money."

エ Indians seem to be short of time.

② ア At the airline company, the clerks were making plans for holidays.

イ At the airline company, the clerks were enjoying their work.

ウ At the airline company, the clerks were doing their work slowly.

エ The clerks were taking time in coming to the office.

③ ア The writer succeeded in getting to his friend's place with some difficulty.

イ The writer headed for his friend's place in order to stay.

ウ The writer failed to find the street where his friend's house stood.

エ The writer tried to look for the way leading to his friend's place.

④ ア A telegram sent by the writer did not arrive as expected.

イ The writer received a telegram from his friend in Bombay to meet him.

ウ The writer's friend in Bombay was surprised to learn that the telegram was delayed so much.

エ An Indian friend came to see the writer at the Bombay airport.

⑤ ア In the end, the writer came to prefer Japanese life to Indian life.

イ Finally, the writer became unconscious of time through some experiences which he had in India.

ウ In conclusion, the writer became interested in the difference of the idea of time between India and Japan.

エ At last, the writer came to dislike the inconvenience of Indian life.

☆ (2) 下線部(a)，(b)を日本語に直せ。(3点×2)

| (a) | |
| (b) | |

In general, human beings regard insects as enemies rather than allies, and scientists spend a greater part of their time fighting the seemingly limitless variety of problems caused by insects. But there is ①another side to the picture. In some cases insects can be used to destroy or limit the spread of troublesome weeds.

5　　Human beings have learnt to their enormous cost the danger of upsetting the natural balance within local communities by importing non-native plants or wild animals. The introduction of the rabbit into Australia is a (a)notorious example of this: less well known is the almost equally serious importation into Australia of prickly-pear cacti. Both rabbits and cacti had no apparent enemies to keep them in check: as a result they
10　multiplied (b)prodigiously and developed into very serious problems. (　A　) both cases their eventual suppression was due mainly to the importation of insects —— the mosquito that spread a fatal disease among rabbits, and the moth that cleared the cacti.

　　The many species of the prickly-pear cacti are all natives of South and Central America. They are useful as hedging plants and their fruits are (c)edible, and
15　(　B　) these reasons they have been introduced into many parts of the world, often with unfortunate results. In Australia the plants found both the climate and the soil suitable, and they quickly began to spread. At the peak of the invasion, in 1919, about 60 million acres of fertile land had been rendered useless and the cacti were estimated to be spreading (　C　) a million acres a year.

20　　In 1920, scientists were sent to investigate insects connected with the prickly pear. Altogether 145 different insects were found, all of them dependent for food on prickly pear or other kinds of cacti.

　　Quite a number of them had to be rejected because it was found that they could also sustain themselves (　D　) tomatoes, peaches, apples, figs and bananas. About 18
25　②'safe' species were finally selected for trials. Several of these managed to establish themselves in Australia, and one species, a moth from Argentina became the most important enemy of the prickly pear.

　　By 1935 almost all the cacti had been destroyed, roots and all. Since then the moth has decreased to a mere fraction of its former numbers owing (　E　) the shortage of
30　prickly pear. But it retains its capacity for rapid increase when conditions are favorable, and so continues as a natural control of the prickly pear. The lost acres have been (d)reclaimed and now in full use for grazing and farming.

(L. Hugh Newman, <u>Man and Insects</u>による)

(注) prickly-pear cacti「ウチワサボテン」(サボテン(cactus)の一種)　　　　　　[聖心女子大]

(1) 本文中の空所（　A　）～（　E　）に入れるのに最も適当な語を次のア～オの中から選び，それぞれ記号で答えよ。ただし同じものを二度使わないこと。(2点×5)

ア　at　　イ　for　　ウ　in　　エ　on　　オ　to

(A) [　　　]　　(B) [　　　]　　(C) [　　　]　　(D) [　　　]　　(E) [　　　]

(2) 下線部(a)～(d)の語の文中の意味として最も適当なものをア～エの中から1つずつ選び，記号で答えよ。

(2点×4)

		ア	イ	ウ	エ
(a)	notorious	famous	fashionable	infamous	favorable
(b)	prodigiously	immensely	invisibly	slowly	suddenly
(c)	edible	eatable	poisonous	profitable	remarkable
(d)	reclaim	reject	remain	restore	retain

(a) [　　　]　　(b) [　　　]　　(c) [　　　]　　(d) [　　　]

☆ (3) 本文中の下線部①と②は何を指しているか，それぞれ 20～30 字程度の日本語で説明せよ。(6点×2)

① [　　　　　　　　　　　　　　　　　　　　　　　　　　　　　　　　　　　　]

② [　　　　　　　　　　　　　　　　　　　　　　　　　　　　　　　　　　　　]

(4) 次の問いに英語で答えよ。(6点)

Why was the introduction of the rabbit into Australia a mistake?

— It was a mistake because _____.

[　　　　　　　　　　　　　　　　　　　　　　　　　　　　　　　　　　　　　]

■ notes

2. seemingly「一見すると」　8. importation「輸入」　cacti cactus（サボテン）の複数形
9. keep O in check「O を食い止める，抑える」　11. eventual「結果として起こる」　suppression「抑制」
12. fatal「致命的な」　moth「蛾」　14. hedge「垣根で囲う」　18. fertile「肥沃な」
render O C「O を C（の状態）にする」　24. sustain「（生命などを）維持する」　29. fraction「ごく少量」
32. grazing「放牧」

06

[人 間 ①]
正直さを生み出す2つの要因

時間 30 分

合格 21 点

得点

/29点

月　　日

解答 ▶ 別冊p.6

We're all taught that honesty is the best policy. Telling the truth is important and it's (①) not to steal or cheat your way through life. I would say, 'I am always totally honest' if you asked me how honest I am. That's certainly how I'd like to be … and probably how most people would like to be. But when you look at honesty box
5　schemes, in some situations, people are not as honest as they'd like to think. So, what determines how honest people are?

Honesty boxes are sometimes used to sell products like newspapers at train stations and vegetables at the farmer's gate. You take what you want and you pay by putting your money in a box. Sometimes, similar systems are used for paying a fare on a bus
10　or train. Schemes like this are good because they avoid long queues. But it's a risk for the seller: if someone didn't pay, the seller wouldn't know (②).

Honesty boxes are now part of the online world, too. In 2007, Radiohead decided to sell their new album, *In Rainbows*, by using a digital version of an honesty box. They released the album as a download and a blank price box appeared on the screen saying,
15　'It's up to you'. Most people paid a fair price.

Why, in this case, were most people honest? There are two major factors that determine how honest people are. Firstly, people are more honest if they think someone is watching them. To test this theory, some researchers did an experiment. A poster was put above an honesty box for tea and coffee in an office and two different
20　posters were tested: one with some flowers and the other with a pair of eyes. The results showed that when the poster was a pair of eyes, people were more honest than when it was some flowers. They clearly felt that someone was watching them.

The second factor is (③): people are more honest when they care about the seller in some way. It could be that people buying the Radiohead album were loyal
25　customers and true fans of Radiohead. To test this idea, in another experiment, shoppers were given too much change. Most people check their change and know when they are given too much or too less. The results of the tests showed that in large supermarkets people usually kept the extra change. In small shops, however, people were more honest and gave it back. So, what about you? Are you as honest as you'd
30　like to be?

[近畿大-改]

■ notes

1. best policy「最善の策」 2. cheat *one's* way「ズルをする」 5. scheme「仕組み」 10. queue「列」
12. Radiohead「レディオヘッド(=英国のロックバンド)」

(1) 空所①〜③に入れるのに最も適切なものをア〜エから１つ選べ。(4点×3)

① ア dispensable 　　イ essential 　　ウ innate 　　エ refined

② ア what did that customer buy 　　イ what that customer bought

　 ウ who was that customer 　　エ who that customer was

③ ア judgment 　　イ privilege 　　ウ loyalty 　　エ specialty

①　[　　]　②　[　　]　③　[　　]

(2) 下線部の内容として最も適当なものを，ア〜エから１つ選べ。(5点)

ア Customers' loyalty to sellers has a large effect on how much customers like sellers.

イ If customers purchased the Radiohead album, it implies that they are more loyal than others.

ウ Loyal Radiohead fans are ones who buy the Radiohead album at a proper price.

エ When customers have a positive feeling toward the seller, they are more honest in their dealings with that vendor.

[　　]

☆ (3) 本文の内容と合わないものを，ア〜キから２つ選べ。ただし，記号（ア，イ，ウ，...）の順序は問わない。(6点×2)

ア In regard to honesty box schemes, people, in some situations, can be less honest than they perceive themselves to be.

イ Food such as vegetables at the farmer's gate can be purchased by using honesty boxes.

ウ A scheme similar to the honesty box at the farmer's gate has never been tried in the payment of fares for public transportation.

エ The blank price box used to download Radiohead's album, *In Rainbows*, resulted in most customers paying a reasonable price.

オ It can be inferred from the results of an experiment that making people feel like they are being watched improves their behavior.

カ The experiment involving two different posters proved that loyalty is one of the two major factors that determine how honest people are.

キ As compared with those of large stores, customers of small shops displayed a greater tendency to return extra change.

[　　|　　]

①Some adults who do not go to college or university when they leave school may wish to do so later in life but find they cannot because of work or family commitments or lack of money. Open learning schemes enable people to take educational courses at any level through part-time study at home when it is convenient for them. Open
5 learning is sometimes called distance learning because most students do not go to an educational institution for classes but study in their own home.

At an informal level, open learning may include learning a language through watching television programs and studying an associated coursebook. Open learning leading to professional qualifications and degrees is often based on ②correspondence
10 courses, though such courses existed before the term *open learning* became popular in the 1970s. Students taking correspondence courses receive printed materials through the post and send essays to a tutor to be marked. On other postal courses students receive all the course material at once and work through it entirely by themselves. Some courses are now offered through the Internet or by subscription to a series of
15 television programs. Although students have to pay to do the courses, the total cost is much less than if they were to give up work to study full-time.

The best-known open learning institution in Britain is the Open University, which was founded in 1969. It accepts students from Britain and from other countries in the European Union. Students can be of any age and,(③), they take a preparatory
20 course before starting their degree. Teaching is by a mixture of printed materials, and television and radio programs. Students study at home and post their work to their tutors. Many go to monthly tutorials at study centers in their hometown, and they may also attend summer schools. Most students take part-time degree courses lasting four or five years, though there is no time limit. Postgraduate and professional courses are
25 also offered. By the mid-1990s the Open University had around 200,000 students and its success has led to similar organizations being set up in other parts of the world.

Although the U.S. has no national institution like the Open University, ④the principle that further education should be open to everyone is widely accepted and there are many opportunities. Many universities and colleges operate correspondence courses,
30 and most, especially those run by state governments, have some means by which interested people can study at university.

［龍谷大-改］

■ notes

3. scheme「計画」　6. educational institution「教育施設」　8. associate「～を関連づける」　10. term「用語」
12. tutor「指導教員」　14. by subscription「予約で」　18. found「～を設立する」　22. tutorial「個人授業」
24. postgraduate「大学院の」　29. operate「～を運営する」　30. run「～を運営する」

(1) 下線部① Some adults で始まる第1文の内容と一致するものを1つ選べ。(6点)

ア 大人になって再び勉強しようと思う人は，聴講生制度を利用する。

イ 大人になって大学で勉強しようとするために最も重要なのは，本人のやる気である。

ウ 大人になって大学で勉強しようと思っても，経済的理由でそうできない人もいる。

エ 大人になって再び勉強しようと思っても大学入学は不可能で，通信教育で学ぶしか
ない。

(2) 下線部②の説明として，本文の内容と一致しないものを1つ選べ。(6点)

ア テレビ番組を見て学習する。

イ インターネットを通じて学習する。

ウ 送料は必要だが教材費は無料である。

エ 郵送された教材を学習し課題を提出する。

(3) 空所③に入れるのに最も適当なものを1つ選べ。(6点)

ア if they do not have the standard qualifications for entering university

イ if they do not have enough money to go to the Open University

ウ if they live far away from the Open University

エ if they want to take courses broadcast on television

☆ (4) 下線部④を日本語に訳せ。(6点)

☆ (5) 本文の内容と一致するものを1つ選べ。(6点)

ア Any adult can study for free in either Britain or the U.S.

イ The principle that adult education should be open to everybody is accepted both in Britain
and the U.S.

ウ Correspondence courses are not included in open learning.

エ Open learning is an educational opportunity unique to the European Union.

☆ (6) 本文の表題として最も適当なものを1つ選べ。(6点)

ア Continuing Education　　イ Classical Education

ウ Compulsory Education　　エ Elementary Education

Philosopher Thomas Nagel once asked, "What is it like to be a bat?" Well, we can try to imagine it. It's dark. We hear a lot of squeaking. We fly. We feel a little bit ... batty. But wait. (a)Does the bat have any sense of its batness? For that matter, what's going on in the mind of a dog, a cow, an ape? Are animals self-aware?

5　One day in the 1960s, while shaving in front of a mirror, psychologist Gordon Gallup wondered what would happen if you put animals in front of a looking glass. He created what he called the mark test, in which apes already familiar with mirrors and their own reflection were drugged and marked with a dye above an eyebrow and on an ear. When the animals woke up, they were shown their reflection in the mirror.

10　Two species, chimpanzees and orangutans, reacted by touching the dyed spots — evidence, Gallup argued, that these species are self-aware. But Donald Griffin, a biologist at Harvard University, thinks other species are also self-aware, even if (b)they haven't passed the mark test. It doesn't (c)make sense, says Griffin, that chimpanzees and orangutans succeed at the test, while other apes, like gorillas, do not. Besides, 15 only 75 percent of adult chimpanzees pass the test. "You'd have to say that some chimpanzees are self-aware and others aren't, which seems a bit ridiculous," Griffin says.

Some researchers believe that dolphins can pass a variation of Gallup's mark test, but (d)it's tricky when all the animal has to work with is a flipper. (e)Hardly anything in 20 this field is free of controversy.

(f)At issue is the degree to which humans are different from other creatures. Are we special, or just self-centered?

Daniel Povinelli, a scientist at the University of Louisiana, argues that even small children who pass the mark test lack the kind of self-awareness that older children 25 have. In one of Povinelli's experiments, kids watch a video of someone secretly placing a large, brightly colored sticker on top of their heads just minutes earlier. Most three-year-olds, upon seeing the video, fail to reach up and remove the sticker. They recognize themselves, but don't quite grasp that the sticker is still on their heads. And yet most four-year-olds pass the test.

30　It is hard to say for certain what the mark test really measures. Research on consciousness and self-awareness is filled with unknowns. Is it possible that some animals, for example, fail the test simply because they lack the proper muscle to touch the mark? Sometimes in science we get interesting answers, but we can't quite decide what it was that we asked.

（注）ape「類人猿」　drug「〜に麻酔をかける」　　　　　　　　　　　　　　［西南学院大-改］

(1) 下線部(a)の意味に最も近いものを，**ア〜エ**から選べ。(4点)

    ア Does the bat have a natural ability to smell?

    イ Does the bat understand its importance?

    ウ Does the bat recognize its calling?

    エ Does the bat have any self-awareness?

(2) 下線部(b)が指すものを**ア〜エ**から選べ。(4点)

    ア two species   **イ** the dyed spots

    ウ chimpanzees and orangutans   **エ** other species

(3) 下線部(c)，(f)の意味に最も近いものをそれぞれ**ア〜エ**から選べ。(4点×2)

    (c) make sense   **ア** sound reasonable   **イ** seem responsible

                            ウ feel fortunate   **エ** become reliable

    (f) At issue   **ア** Being born   **イ** Being debated

                            ウ Being disagreeable   **エ** Being published

(4) 下線部(d)，(e)の意味に最も近いものをそれぞれ**ア〜エ**から選べ。(6点×2)

    (d) **ア** それらすべての動物が動くとき，たくみに使えるのはヒレだけである。

          イ その実験は，対象となる動物がヒレしか使えない場合はやっかいである。

          ウ その実験は，対象となる動物がすべてヒレを持つ魚の場合は工夫が必要である。

          エ それらすべての動物は，ヒレしか用いることができないにもかかわらず大変器
             用な行動をする。

    (e) **ア** この研究領域においては，何についてであれ論争は避けがたい。

          イ この研究領域においては，何についてであれ自由に議論することはほとんどない。

          ウ この研究領域においては，何についてであれ自由に意見を言うことができる。

          エ この研究領域においては，何についてであれ論争はほとんどない。

☆ (5) 本文の内容に合うように，次の英文の空所に入れるのに最も適当なものをそれぞれ**ア〜エ**から選べ。

(6点×2)

    ①   A majority of three-year-old children (   ).

        ア are less self-aware than gorillas

        イ perform better than four-year-olds

        ウ don't realize the sticker is on their heads

        エ usually reach up and remove the sticker

    ②   One possible cause for an animal to fail the test might be (   ).

        ア insufficient physical capability   **イ** inability to ask for help

        ウ too much self-awareness   **エ** not enough marks

■ notes

  8. reflection「(自分の)姿」　dye「染料，〜を染める」　10. react「反応する」　28. grasp「〜を理解する」

[歴 史 ①]
女性解放運動

①Today we take it for granted that women have as much right to vote as men have. Women may keep what they earn. Whether married or single, they may own property. It is taken for granted that a woman may go to college and work in any business or profession she may choose. But these rights, enjoyed by the women of today, were
5　secured through the valiant effort of many fighters for women's freedom, and first of all by the great Susan B. Anthony.

　About a hundred years ago, American women could earn money, but they were not allowed to own it. If a woman was married and went to work, every penny she earned became the property of her husband. He was considered complete master of the
10　household. His wife was considered a nitwit unable to think clearly, and therefore the law mercifully protected her by appointing a guardian —— a male guardian, of course —— over any property she was lucky enough to possess.

　Women like Susan Anthony were furious at this injustice. Susan saw no reason why women should be treated that way.

15　On Election Day in 1872, fifteen women including Susan gathered at a storefront. "I've come here to vote for the President of the United States," she said. "He will be my President as well as yours. We are the women who bear the children who will defend this country. We are the women who make your homes, who cook your meals, who rear your sons and daughters. We women are citizens of this country just as much as
20　you are, and we insist on voting for the man who is to be our leader."

　Her words ②rang out with the clearness of a bell, and they struck to the heart. And then, in silence and dignity, Susan strode up to the ballot box and dropped into it the paper bearing her vote. Each of the other fourteen women did the same.

　On that important day in 1872, Susan B. Anthony and her faithful followers
25　symbolically cast their first ballots for the President of the United States. She was America's greatest champion of women's rights.

[梅花女子大]

■ notes

5. secure「〜を手に入れる」 valiant「勇敢な」 10. nitwit「ばか，うすのろ」 11. mercifully「寛大に」
13. be furious at 〜「〜に激怒する」 injustice「不公平」 19. rear「〜を育てる」
20. insist on doing「〜することを主張[要求]する」 22. strode stride(つかつかと歩く)の過去形
ballot「投票」

★ (1) 次の①〜③において，本文の内容に最もよく合っているものを，それぞれア〜エから１つずつ選べ。

(6 点× 3)

① ア About a hundred years ago, women were not allowed to work to earn money.

   イ In those days women could not own a single penny they earned.

   ウ Married women who went to work in those days were not allowed to stay in their husbands' property.

   エ Women in those days, whether married or single, could own property.

② ア Susan was reluctant to fight for women's freedom.

   イ Women like Susan took no action to challenge the social injustice which treated women so unfairly.

   ウ Women like Susan stood up to challenge unfair treatment of women.

   エ Susan fought for women's freedom without any followers.

③ ア What Susan meant in her words was a call for "more homes and more meals."

   イ What Susan wanted to say in her words was "The President should be for women, not for men."

   ウ What Susan really wanted to say was "Women are the best and strongest."

   エ What Susan was eager to say was that women should participate in voting for the leader of the whole nation.

★ (2) 下線部①，②を和訳せよ。(4 点× 2)

①	
②	

　　The Japanese often claim that "there are terrible traffic jams because Japan is small and there are too many cars." However, the situation is just the same in any of the world's large cities. Places like Bangkok, Beijing, Mexico City, and Athens are famed for traffic jams and exhaust gas, and there seems to be no end to the problem.

5　　Singapore has cleverly dealt (　A　) this situation by putting a transit tax on all cars in the center of the city. During the daytime, drivers who want to enter the area pay at a toll booth and get a card which they stick on their windshield. If you should enter without paying the fee, one of the toll booth operators will note down your license plate number, and you will (a)be fined later.

10　　Because the government of Singapore has,(　B　) the first place, put a limit on (　①　) number of cars in the country, people who want to buy a car must wait until they can get an owner's permit. (　②　), the cost of owning a car, including permit money, taxes, and the car itself, can amount to ten million yen. On top of this, gasoline is very expensive, about twice the price in neighboring Malaysia. Even so, it seems

15 many Singaporeans still want to own a car.

　　Even if the situation is not so strict in other countries, many (　③　) have some form of traffic control system. In Jakarta, Indonesia, if you go on the main roads during the day, you must have at least three people in the car, including the driver. In order to fulfill this head count, the part-time job of being the "third person" has appeared.

20　　Athens, the Greek capital, is famous (　C　) the ancient Parthenon temple, but since it is located near the center of the city, this temple is being damaged by exhaust gas. (b)In this city there is a system regulating vehicle use according to whether the last digit of your license plate is odd or even, but it seems to have had little effect.

　　Australia is a country where it is inconvenient (　D　) a car. To cut down the

25 number of cars, the government introduced "transit lanes," which give priority to cars with more than two passengers. After this system was established, though, some people have complained that while they do pick up a neighbor (　E　) the way, the one-way trip to that neighbor's house may take an extra thirty minutes.

　　In Japan, such traffic systems do not yet exist, but on seeing the inconveniences they

30 cause in other countries, it is difficult to decide whether or not such regulations should be introduced.

（注）toll booth「料金所」　windshield「（車の）フロントガラス」　owner's permit「所有許可証」

　　　Parthenon temple「パルテノン神殿」　digit「数字」

[東邦大]

(1) 空所(A)〜(E)を埋めるのに最も適当な語を1つずつ選べ。同じものは2度は使えない。

ア without　　イ with　　ウ in　　エ for　　オ on

(A)　　　　(B)　　　　(C)　　　　(D)　　　　(E)

(2) 空所①〜③を埋めるのに最も適当な語(句)を1つずつ選べ。(4 点×3)

① ア a　　　　イ the　　　　ウ even　　　　エ odd
② ア Finally　　イ Thirdly　　ウ In addition　　エ On the contrary
③ ア did　　　イ do　　　　ウ does　　　　エ will

①　　　　②　　　　③

(3) 下線部(a)の意味に最も近いものを選べ。(4 点)

ア 発見される　　イ 逮捕される　　ウ 元気になる　　エ 罰金を科される

☆ (4) 下線部(b)を和訳せよ。(6 点)

(5) 本文の内容と一致するものを2つ選べ。(6 点× 2)

ア Among the cities mentioned, Bangkok is the only one that does not suffer from terrible traffic jams.

イ In Jakarta, you could earn money just by riding a car.

ウ In Athens, air pollution is causing damage to an ancient temple.

エ In Australia, the system of "transit lanes" is supported by everyone.

23

You carry around a three-pound (1.4 kg) mass of wrinkly material in your head that controls every single thing you will ever do. From enabling you to think, learn, create, and feel emotions to controlling every blink, breath, and heartbeat —— this fantastic control center is your brain. It is a structure so (a)amazing that a famous scientist once
5　called it "the most ①complex thing we have yet discovered in our universe."

Your cat is on the kitchen counter. She's about to step onto a hot stove. You have only seconds to act. Accessing the signals coming from your eyes, your brain quickly calculates when, where, and at what speed you will need to dive to catch her. Then it orders your muscles to do so. Your timing is perfect and she's safe. No computer can
10　come close to your brain's remarkable ability to download, process, and react to the flood of information coming from your eyes, ears, and other sensory organs.

Your brain contains about 100 billion neurons —— so many that it would take you over 3,000 years to count them all. Whenever you dream, laugh, think, see, or move, it's because tiny chemical and electrical signals are racing between these neurons
15　along billions of tiny neuron highways. Believe it or (A), the activity in your brain never stops. Countless messages travel around inside it every second like a supercharged pinball machine. Your neurons create and send more messages than all the phones in the ②entire world. And while a single neuron produces only a tiny amount of electricity, all your neurons together can produce enough electricity to
20　power a low-wattage bulb.

A bee lands on your ③bare foot. Sensory neurons in your skin relay this information to your spinal cord and brain at a speed of more than 150 miles (240 km) per hour. Your brain then uses motor neurons to send the message back through your spinal cord to your foot to shake the bee off quickly. Motor neurons can relay this
25　information at more than 200 miles (320 km) per hour.

Riding a bike seems (B) at first. But soon you master it. How? As you practice, your brain sends "bike riding" messages along certain pathways of neurons over and (C), forming new connections. In fact, the structure of your brain changes every time you learn, as well as whenever you have a new thought or memory.
30　It is well known that any exercise that makes your heart beat faster, like running or playing basketball, is great for your body and can even help improve your mood. But scientists have recently learned that for a period of time after you've exercised, your body produces a chemical that makes your brain more receptive to learning. So if you're stuck on a homework problem, go out and play a game of soccer, then try the
35　problem again. You just might discover that you're able to solve it.

(注) wrinkly「しわの多い」　sensory organ「感覚器官」　neuron「神経細胞」
　　supercharged pinball machine「勢いづいたピンボールゲーム機」　low-wattage bulb「低ワット数の電球」
　　spinal cord「脊髄(せきずい)」　stuck「行き詰まって」

［東京経済大］

(1) 空所（　A　）～（　C　）を埋めるのに最も適当な語を1つずつ選べ。(2点×3)

　(A)　ア seeing　　　イ not　　　ウ never　　　エ unbelievable
　(B)　ア fun　　　　イ easy　　　ウ exhausting　　　エ impossible
　(C)　ア above　　　イ done　　　ウ over　　　エ out

(A) ☐　　(B) ☐　　(C) ☐

(2) 下線部①～③の意味に最も近いものを1つずつ選べ。(4点×3)

　①　ア simplistic　　イ theatrical　　ウ inferior　　エ complicated
　②　ア whole　　　　イ tiresome　　　ウ encircled　　エ entry-level
　③　ア candid　　　　イ bear-like　　　ウ naked　　　エ athlete's

① ☐　　② ☐　　③ ☐

(3) 下線部(a)とほぼ同じ意味の1語を第2段落から1つ選んで書け。(4点)

☐

☆ (4) 本文の内容と一致するものを2つ選べ。(6点×2)

　ア After doing physical exercises, your brain does not function very well.
　イ When you are asleep, your brain activity stops for a short period of time.
　ウ Motor neurons can relay information faster than sensory neurons.
　エ To feel emotions, your brain is indispensable.

☐ ☐

■ notes
1. mass「かたまり」　3. blink「まばたき」　6. stove「コンロ」　10. process「～を処理する」
14. chemical「化学物質」　race「高速で走る」　23. motor neuron「運動神経」
31. improve「～を改善する」　(4) エ. indispensable「必要不可欠の」

Why a language becomes a global language ①has little to do with the number of people who speak it. ②It is much more to do with who those speakers are. Latin became an international language throughout the Roman Empire, but this was not because the Romans were more numerous than the people they conquered. They were simply more powerful. Later, when Roman military power declined, Latin remained for a millennium as the international language of education, ③thanks to a different sort of power — the religious power of Roman Catholicism.

There is also the closest of links between language dominance and economic, technological, and cultural power. Without a strong power-base, of whatever kind, no language can make progress as an international medium of communication. Language has no independent existence, living in some sort of mystical space ④apart from the people who speak it. Language exists only in the brains and mouths and ears and hands and eyes of its users. When they succeed on the international stage, their language succeeds. When they fail, their language fails.

This point may seem obvious, but it needs to be made, because over the years many ⑤popular and misleading beliefs have grown up about why a language should become internationally successful. It is quite common to hear people claim that an international language is an ideal model, on account of its literary qualities and clarity of expression. Hebrew, Greek, Latin, Arabic and French are among those which at various times have been praised in such terms, and English is no exception. It is often suggested, for example, that there must be something inherently beautiful or logical about the structure of English, in order to explain why it is now so widely used. "It has less grammar than other languages," some have suggested. This is intended to mean that the language is grammatically not so complicated compared with other languages, so ⑥it must be easier to learn.

Such arguments are misconceived. Latin was once a major international language, despite the fact that it seems grammatically much more complicated. ⑦A language does not become a global language because of its intrinsic structural properties, or because of the size of its vocabulary, or because it has been a vehicle of a great literature in the past, or because it was once associated with a great culture or religion. A language has traditionally become an international language for one chief reason: the power of its people — especially their political and military power.

［学習院大-改］

■ notes
4. numerous「多数の」 8. dominance「優位(性)」 21. inherently「本質的に」 26. argument「主張」
misconceive「思い違いをする」 28. intrinsic「本来備わっている」 29. vehicle「伝達手段」

(1) 下線部①，③，④の意味に最も近いものをそれぞれア～エから選べ。(4点×3)

① ア is not compatible with　　イ is not connected with
　 ウ is not content with　　　エ is not important to

③ ア owing to　　　イ in gratitude to
　 ウ in terms of　　エ with respect to

④ ア depending on　　イ distinct from
　 ウ except for　　　エ independent of

①	③	④

(2) 下線部②が指している語句の最初と最後の単語を書け。(4点)

最初 [　　　　　] 　　最後 [　　　　　]

☆ (3) 下線部⑤の内容を最も端的に表している箇所を本文中から探し，句読点を含め40字以内の日本語に訳せ。(6点)

(4) 下線部⑥の it が表す具体的なものを本文中から1語選んで書け。(4点)

(5) 下線部⑦の意味に最も近いものをア～エから選べ。(6点)

ア A language does not become a global language, for it has intrinsic structural problems.

イ Because of its intrinsic structural properties, a language does not become a global language.

ウ It is because of intrinsic properties that a language does not become a global language.

エ It is not because of intrinsic properties that a language becomes a global language.

☆ (6) 本文から判断して，ある言語が international language になる要因と思われるものを次のア～カから3つ選べ。(6点×3)

ア the governmental power of its users' countries

イ the high level of the technology of its users

ウ the large population of its users

エ the long tradition of literature it has produced

オ the military potential of the countries where it is used

カ the simplicity of its grammar

Social media is fuelling an eating disorder in which people focus so closely on eating "healthy" food that they become unwell. Diet experts say that orthorexia, a constant need to eat food that sufferers consider to be "healthy" or "correct" for them, is a growing problem thanks to the promotion of clean eating and wellness on sites such as Instagram. Rather than becoming a picture of health, many people are ①restricting their diets so much that they become unhealthy and ②starved of vital substances needed for heath and growth, resulting in weight loss, weakness and decreasing bone strength.

Orthorexia is not officially recognised but was coined in 1997 by the American doctor and author Steven Bratman. Research by Cristina Bresch of the University of Sciences, Philadelphia, shows that most sufferers follow Instagram users showing an idealised lifestyle based on eating an exclusively healthy diet. "People have always tried to eat healthily, that's nothing new," Dr. Bresch said. "But what we are seeing now is people becoming concerned with clean eating to the point where it affects both their physical and mental health, and that's something we've never seen before." She said that the combination of the "wellness trend" and the speed and reach of social media had helped to produce orthorexia. "Seeing images on social media of unrealistically attractive people looking happy, who ③claim that they got there through so-called 'healthy' eating, then makes these more easily-led people buy into that lifestyle too."

Evidence is ④due to be submitted to the *Diagnostic and Statistical Manual of Mental Disorders* to make the case for orthorexia to be recognised officially. Renee McGregor, a British registered diet expert, said that the present process for identifying the illness was loosely based and rested largely on the extent to which the patient's eating habits had an impact on the person's health. "It's very difficult to recognise as it is not always linked to weight or body image," she said. "It's more a psychological urge and an inability to moderate their diet. They just physically can't eat something like a pizza or cake. More and more, I'm seeing people come forward realising they have a problem. Typically, these people follow unqualified Insta-stars, who in actual fact are promoting a very dangerous way of eating. It's almost like a religion."

（注）*Diagnostic and Statistical Manual of Mental Disorders*　アメリカ精神医学会が発行する『精神疾患の診断・統計マニュアル』

[甲南大-改]

■ notes
1. fuel「〜をあおる」　eating disorder「摂食障害」　4. wellness「健康であること」　6. vital「必須の」
9. coin「(新語などを)作り出す」　12. idealised = idealized「理想的な」　exclusively「もっぱら」
17. unrealistically「非現実的に」　20. submit「〜を提出する」　26. inability「できないこと」
moderate「〜を加減する」　28. unqualified「資格のない」

(1) 下線部①〜④に代わる語句として最も適切なものを選択肢から選べ。(4点×4)

① ア consuming　イ expanding　ウ limiting　エ purchasing

② ア conscious of　イ lacking in　ウ made of　エ uninterested in

③ ア assert　イ complain　ウ deny　エ doubt

④ ア allowed　イ expected　ウ likely　エ ready

☆ (2) 第1, 2パラグラフの内容と一致するものを選択肢から2つ選べ。(6点×2)

ア In contrast to most people's wish to eat healthily, they are encouraged by social media to eat foods that are essentially bad for them.

イ According to diet experts, people are becoming more and more aware of what kinds of health problems are due to viewing posts on Instagram.

ウ Cristina Bresch found that people with orthorexia are often influenced by the images in which a focus on eating only healthy foods is at the centre of an ideal lifestyle.

エ According to Bresch, a new phenomenon is emerging in which, paradoxically, people are so worried about having a healthy lifestyle that they run into difficulties, both physical and mental.

オ Bresch argues that thanks to the rapid spread of social media, the number of people suffering from orthorexia has been reduced.

☆ (3) 第3パラグラフの内容と一致するものを選択肢から1つ選べ。(6点)

ア Renee McGregor argues that when it comes to identifying orthorexia, there is no correlation between a patient's daily diet and the person's mental or physical condition.

イ McGregor argues that the cause of orthorexia often lies in mental states and cannot necessarily be judged by a patient's outward appearance.

ウ According to McGregor, Insta-stars have begun to be aware that their way of encouraging people to eat a larger quantity of junk food than they can consume is highly problematic.

エ McGregor argues that people who admire Insta-stars are really recommending a harmful diet as a symbol of their faith.

　　In the early 19th century, as Americans began writing the history of their fight for independence from the British, they looked for heroes and heroines who symbolized the spirit of the nation. There were many male figures to fill the lead role in their national drama. George Washington, who served as first President of the United
5　States, was the clear choice as "Father of the Nation." However, there was no ①obvious female lead character. A number of women played significant parts in America's independence drama, such as Washington's wife, Martha; Betsy Ross, the woman credited with making the "Stars and Stripes" flag; and Esther Berdt Reed, a patriotic Philadelphia housewife. However, these women's contributions were mostly away from
10　the fighting. What historians were really looking for was a battlefield heroine. They eventually turned their attention to the ②dimly remembered story of Mary Hays, a Pennsylvania woman who followed Washington's army to care for her soldier husband. She later became known as the legendary "Molly Pitcher," America's Revolutionary War heroine.
15　　Mary was born in 1744 in colonial New Jersey to German immigrants. There she was raised until she was sixteen, when she moved to the town of Carlisle in Pennsylvania to take up a position as a domestic servant in the home of a Dr. Irvine. According to public records, in 1769 she married a barber called William Hays, an immigrant from Ireland. Mary and William led a normal married life in Carlisle until
20　1777, when Dr. Irvine organized a group of volunteer soldiers to fight in the War for Independence as part of Washington's army. William was one of the first to enlist.
　　With her husband in the army, Mary became a "camp follower," one of a group of soldiers' wives led by Martha Washington, who would bake and deliver food, wash clothes and blankets, and care for sick and dying soldiers. (a)In the camp, she quickly
25　became known as Molly, a common nickname for Mary. In the spring of 1778, William was trained as an artilleryman, a man whose job was to load and fire cannons. Mary then began serving as a "water girl" carrying pitchers — buckets — of fresh water to the artillerymen who needed it both to drink and to cool down the hot cannons. Mary Hays would eventually become known as "Molly Pitcher" from the cries of men on the
30　battlefield calling out "Molly! Pitcher!" when they needed water.
　　On June 28, 1778, Washington's army attacked the British army that had captured the town of Monmouth Courthouse in New Jersey. Mary was with her husband's unit, serving as a water girl. The weather that day was ③incredibly hot. Sometime during the battle William collapsed next to his cannon, exhausted by the heat. As her husband
35　was carried off the battlefield, Mary took his place loading and firing the cannon for the rest of the day. At one point, the story goes, a British bullet tore through the bottom

of her skirt. She supposedly dismissed it saying, "That could have been worse," then continued to load the cannon. After the battle, Washington was so impressed by her courage that he made Mary an honorary officer in his army.

［南山大-改］

(1) アメリカ独立戦争で活躍した女性の中で，Molly Pitcher が Betsy Ross，Esther Berdt Reed たちと大きく異なっている点は何か，15 字以内の日本語で書け。(4 点)

[　　　　　　　　　　　　　　　　　　　　　　　　　　　　　]

(2) 下線部①〜③の意味に最も近いものを 1 つずつ選べ。(4 点×3)

① ア brave　　　イ clear　　　ウ oblivious　　　エ pretty
② ア bitterly　　イ beautifully　ウ vaguely　　　エ clearly
③ ア extremely　イ predictably　ウ mildly　　　エ somewhat

① □　　② □　　③ □

☆ (3) 下線部(a)を和訳せよ。(6 点)

[　　　　　　　　　　　　　　　　　　　　　　　　　　　　　]

☆ (4) 本文の内容と一致するものには T，一致しないものには F を書け。(4 点×6)

(A) Molly was born in Germany.
(B) Molly's husband was an immigrant.
(C) Martha Washington was the leader of "camp followers."
(D) Molly was called "Molly Pitcher" because she carried pitchers.
(E) Molly took the place of her husband because he was killed in the battle.
(F) George Washington shrugged off the courage of Molly.

(A) □　　(B) □　　(C) □

(D) □　　(E) □　　(F) □

■ notes

8. patriotic「愛国心の強い」　20. volunteer soldier「義勇兵」　22. camp follower「非戦闘従軍者」
26. cannon「大砲」　39. honorary officer「名誉将校」

　　Parents are a child's first teachers. But some parents never learned from good examples. In New York City, a nonprofit agency called Covenant House tries to help homeless young mothers become good parents.

　　The twelve or so teenage mothers who live at the shelter (　A　) parenting classes
5　four days a week. The class is called Mommy and Me. Teacher Delores Clemens is a mother of five and a grandmother. She teaches basic skills, like how to give a baby a bath and how to dress a baby depending on the season. She remembers one student who learned from her mother not to pick up a crying baby. The mother said that would only make the child needy and overly ①demanding.

10　Clemens says: "I said, 'That's not true. You have to hold your baby! He is crying for a reason. If you never pick him up, he's going to keep crying. Pick your baby up. Cuddle your baby. Hug him!' And she started to do that. They just want a little cuddling and a little love. And it works!" She says her students also learn how to be good mothers by letting themselves be mothered. Clemens concludes, "I'm doing
15　something for them that never has been done for them before."

　　Around 350 teenage mothers graduate from Covenant House's Mommy and Me class every year. In class on this day, with her baby son, is Natasha. She lived on the streets. She is glad not (　B　) for the warmth and shelter of Covenant House, but, as she told reporter Adam Phillips, she is also glad for the help they offer in seeking
20　a more ②secure life. Natasha says, "They help you do your resume, your cover letter and everything you need for a job interview, and they help you find a job in whatever you're interested in."

REPORTER: "Did you go to high school?"

NATASHA: "Yes, I did."

25　REPORTER: "Did you graduate?"

NATASHA: "No, I didn't. I was in my last year and then, I got pregnant and I got lazy."

REPORTER: "You look like you are willing to accept responsibility for that."

NATASHA: "Yes, I am, and I want to finish."

　　(a)Some teenage mothers wish they could be children themselves again. Eighteen-
30　year-old Placida knows that feeling. She says being a mom is hard. "Because you have to get up (　C　) two hours in the middle of the night, and you can't go out and say, 'I am going to buy this for myself.' No. I have to buy Pampers, clothes and food. So now it's two. It's not only one. So it's very hard."

The World Health Organization says the United States has forty-one births for every one thousand girls age fifteen to nineteen. (b)That is higher than other developed countries, as well as some developing ones. By comparison, northern neighbor Canada has fourteen births.

(注) cuddle「～を抱き締める」 resume「履歴書」 ［京都橘大］

(1) 空所（ A ）～（ C ）を埋めるのに最も適当な語を1つずつ選べ。(2点×3)

(A) ア attend　　イ extend　　ウ intend　　エ pretend

(B) ア little　　イ only　　ウ much　　エ a lot

(C) ア only　　イ every　　ウ after　　エ over

(A) ☐　　(B) ☐　　(C) ☐

(2) 下線部①，②の意味に最も近いものを1つずつ選べ。(4点×2)

① ア careful　　イ calm　　ウ insistent　　エ obedient

② ア stable　　イ stalled　　ウ secret　　エ secular

① ☐　　② ☐

☆ (3) 下線部(a)，(b)を和訳せよ。(6点×2)

(a) _____

(b) _____

☆ (4) 本文の内容と一致するものを2つ選べ。(6点×2)

ア Covenant House is trying to attract many teenage mothers to make money.

イ Delores Clemens has as many as five children.

ウ Before coming to Covenant House, Natasha was homeless.

エ About 350 babies are born in Covenant House every year.

オ Placida thinks being a mother is a lot of fun.

☐ ☐

■ notes

4. shelter「シェルター，一時保護施設」　20. cover letter「カバーレター（＝履歴書に添えて出す手紙）」

Michael was six years old when he saw a TV programme about rabbits which made him want to own one very much. Every day he kept saying to his mother, "Can I have a rabbit, please, Mom?" and when she made (①), "Why can't I have one?"

His mother knew that when small children have pets, it is their parents who have
5 to look after them most of the time. "You see," she said, "children suddenly become (②) to have a dog, or a rabbit or something, and they think they won't be able to live without it, and that they'll love it and look after it and feed it. But after a few weeks they find other interesting things to do, such as watching TV, and they begin to (③) their pet. Then they have (④) with their parents about it, and the parents will be
10 having to spend more and more time doing what the children should be doing. But, on the other hand, it is a good idea to (⑤) a child from an early age to love animals."

So, finally, on his seventh birthday, Michael's parents bought him not one but two rabbits.

"It's better to have two," his father said to him. "(a)They'll keep each other company
15 when they're left alone." Then he said to his wife, "I hope you made sure they're both boys or both girls: we don't want hundreds of the things in a year's time!"

"Oh, yes," Michael's mother answered. "They're both females." Michael was delighted with the rabbits, and he enjoyed them more and more as they grew up, but they soon became (⑥) to his parents, who had to look after them while Michael
20 was at school.

They tried to think of various ways of (⑦) the rabbits, and finally Michael's father decided that a direct attack would be best, so one day he said to his wife, "(b)What about having one of those rabbits for dinner tonight?"

(A)Michael smiled happily and, before his mother could answer, said, "That would be
25 wonderful, Dad. But do you think she'd be able to hold her spoon?"

They still have the rabbits.

[愛知学院大]

■ notes

1. programme = program「番組」 2. own「～を所有する」 17. female「メス」 21. various「さまざまな」
22. direct attack「ひと思いにやること」 25. hold「～を（手に）持つ，握る」

(1) ①～⑦の空所に入れるのに最も適当なものをア～エの中から1つ選べ。(4点×7)

① ア plans　　　　イ haste　　　　ウ excuses　　　エ an effort

② ア known　　　イ eager　　　　ウ interested　　エ hesitant

③ ア neglect　　　イ miss　　　　 ウ sell　　　　　エ mind

④ ア words　　　 イ a word　　　　ウ word　　　　エ the word

⑤ ア show　　　　イ train　　　　 ウ prevent　　　エ understand

⑥ ア a delight　　イ a boast　　　ウ a nuisance　エ a pity

⑦ ア taking care of　　　 イ being proud of

　 ウ getting rid of　　　 エ becoming familiar with

①	②	③	④

⑤	⑥	⑦

(2) 下線部(A)について，「マイケルがうれしそうに笑った」理由として最も適当な英文をア～エの中から
　 1つ選べ。(6点)

ア He thought his mother was against his father's decision that a direct attack would be best.

イ He thought his father had suggested that a dinner party for his seventh birthday should be
　 held with one rabbit present.

ウ He thought his mother would teach one rabbit to hold her spoon.

エ He thought his father had suggested that they have dinner with one rabbit.

☆ (3) 本文中の下線部(a)，(b)を日本語に直せ。(6点×2)

(a)	
(b)	

One morning, I was teaching little girls in the first-grade classroom. Two of them, very close friends, took out big pieces of paper, and pencils, sat down at a table and got ready to draw. After some thought, one began to draw a very large tree. She started at the bottom of the page and drew two lines, which came close to each other and then
5　went parallel up the page, almost to the very top before they began to spread out again. Then she made a fork in this trunk, near the top. From the two main branches so ①obtained she drew several smaller branches, which she began to cover with leaves. All the while, the other little girl watched, and did nothing. After a while I said to her, 'What are you going to draw?' I did not insist. I was only curious. She said, 'I don't
10　know what to draw.' ②I said, 'Why not draw another tree?' She said, without any hesitation or shame, 'I don't know how.'

　　It was a surprise and revelation to me. Though I like to look at much drawing and painting, I know very little about it. There was almost no art in my own schooling. I can only remember one art class, and one picture that I tried to draw an owl sitting on a
15　limb of a dead tree, with a full moon behind it; for me, a rather ambitious work. I never finished it. As a result of my inexperience, I had the naive idea that artists just look ③(ア at イ front ウ in エ is オ of カ them キ what) and copy it, getting better at this as they go along. Only recently have I learned that to make, with lines and colors, an image that looks like something real, ④takes technique. There is a trick,
20　or many tricks, that have to be learned, practiced, and perfected. We believe that a picture looks like life, but it really doesn't. Pictures are flat, but life is not. It has depth. Therefore, turning real objects into flat pictures needs many tricks, which must be learned.

（注）revelation「意外な発見」　naive「単純な」　　　　　　　　　　　　　　　　［専修大］

6. fork「(木の)また」　trunk「(木の)幹」　9. curious「好奇心の強い」　15. limb「大枝」
19. trick「コツ，秘訣」　21. life「実物」　depth「奥行き」　22. real object「実物」

(1) 下線部①を他の英語に書き換えた場合，最も適当なものを次のア～エの中から１つ選べ。（2点）

　　　ア kept　　イ help　　ウ drawn　　エ taken

(2) 下線部②を I suggested to her that she (　　　) another tree. に書き換えた場合，空所を補うのに最も適当なものを，次のア～エの中から１つ選べ。（4点）

　　　ア draw　　イ drew　　ウ could not draw　　エ should not draw

(3) 下線部③の語順を並べ換えて，正しく意味の通る英文を作れ。答えはア～キの語を(　)と(　)に１つずつ入れて完成させてから，Ⓐ，Ⓑに入れた語の記号を答えよ。（4点×2）

　　　ア at　　イ front　　ウ in　　エ is　　オ of　　カ them　　キ what

　　　(　　　)〔　Ⓐ　〕(　　　)(　　　　)(　　　)〔　Ⓑ　〕(　　　)

(4) 下線部④に最も近い意味を持つ語を含む文を，ア～エから１つ選べ。（4点）

　　　ア Would you take John home?
　　　イ He will probably take first place in the contest.
　　　ウ The mother wanted to take her son in her arms.
　　　エ It will take courage to say such a thing.

☆ (5) 本文の内容と一致するものを，次のア～エの中から２つ選び，その記号を答えよ。解答の順序は問わない。（6点×2）

　　　ア A girl, looking at the big tree, began to copy it on paper with two pencils from the bottom up.
　　　イ The other girl would not draw a picture because there was no tree before her.
　　　ウ The teacher, in his school day, tried to draw a difficult picture, but could not complete it.
　　　エ Now the teacher thinks that an artist needs much practice and skill to change real objects into an image with lines and colors.

I met a farmer named Kenji the other day, but he isn't a typical farmer. Kenji works （　A　） an office building in downtown Tokyo. Like most city people, he rides the subway to work and then takes an elevator to his job. However, unlike those with whom he （　①　） an elevator, Kenji doesn't spend his day straining his eyes in front 5　of a computer screen. Instead, he goes up to the roof and spends his days （　B　） his knees, affectionately caring （　C　） a field of sweet potatoes fifty stories above the ground. When the sunlight fades （　D　） twilight, he changes his clothes and rides the elevator back down to the bright lights and clamor of the big city.

　　This is definitely not the farming job that my grandfather had. Kenji's job has some 10　of the same tasks, but his location and purpose suggest a passion for bringing farming into modern life. In my grandfather's day, the kids left the farm to get good jobs in the city, and very few ever returned. However, nowadays growing food has become more fashionable. There is a certain desire not to go back to the farm but to bring a bit of the farm to the city. In fact, most of my friends in the city grow tomato plants on 15　windowsills or balconies. Now, when people say "farmer," I think of young, cool, urban Kenji, a guy with a little dirt under his fingernails as well as a downtown address.

　　In addition to being fashionable, these rooftop farms benefit residents and the environment. The sweet potatoes across Kenji's roof garden provide food, and their broad leaves also provide shade, which keeps the roof cooler. People in the building do 20　not use air-conditioning as often, so less energy is needed, which （　E　） turn means the air control systems produce less heat and less pollution. It's a win-win situation.

　　The plants also take carbon monoxide from traffic and industry and turn it into good, clean oxygen. This simple yet elegant process for cleaning the air may be a small step, but it is a step in the right （　②　）. If rooftop farms become more popular, cities could 25　soon be covered with oxygen-producing green zones high above the noise and bustle of everyday urban life.

　　In addition to providing environmental benefits, rooftop farms contribute to the economy. Plants need to be （　③　） and watered, and they need someone to pull weeds, so employees like Kenji are paid to help building owners set up and maintain 30　farms on their roofs as well as offer advice on what to plant. (Sweet potatoes are good because they love the hot sun and don't mind the wind.)

　　The employment agency Pasona is hoping that farming ── urban or otherwise ── will become a popular career option. Pasona started an agricultural training program in the basement of their downtown office in Tokyo's Otemachi district. (a)If you 35　walked in the building's front doors, you would never imagine that young people study agriculture there not on the roof, but in the basement. Take the elevator down two floors, and you will see roses blooming, tomato seedlings climbing up their wire frames, and lettuces and pumpkins stretching their leaves toward lights in the ceiling. Another room has rice plants swaying in the breeze created by white-coated workers who wander back and (　④　) between the rooms, pushing buttons and adjusting the climate.

40

(注)clamor「騒々しい音」　carbon monoxide「一酸化炭素」　bustle「喧騒，せわしげな動き」　seedling「苗木」

［佛教大学-改］

(1) 空所(　A　)～(　E　)を埋めるのに最も適当な語を1つずつ選べ。同じものは2度は使えない。

(2点×5)

　　ア in　　**イ** into　　**ウ** on　　**エ** for　　**オ** at

(A) ☐　　(B) ☐　　(C) ☐　　(D) ☐　　(E) ☐

(2) 空所①～④を埋めるのに最も適当な語を1つずつ選べ。(4点×4)

① **ア** divides　　　　**イ** shares　　　　**ウ** co-owns　　　**エ** competes
② **ア** angle　　　　　**イ** foot　　　　　**ウ** below　　　　**エ** direction
③ **ア** food　　　　　　**イ** feed　　　　　**ウ** fed　　　　　**エ** feeding
④ **ア** forth　　　　　　**イ** front　　　　　**ウ** facade　　　　**エ** fringe

① ☐　　② ☐　　③ ☐　　④ ☐

☆ (3) 下線部(a)を和訳せよ。(6点)

☆ (4) 本文の内容と一致するものを2つ選べ。(6点×2)

　　ア The elevator Kenji uses is run by the solar cells on the roof of the building.

　　イ Most of the author's friends in the city grow plants.

　　ウ Thanks to Kenji's farm, the use of electricity by the residents of the building is reduced.

　　エ Sweet potatoes become sweeter if raised on a rooftop farm.

☐ ☐

■ notes

4. strain「～を使いすぎて痛める，酷使する」　15. windowsill「窓台，窓の下枠」　29. weed「雑草」

A Japanese tourist guide was requested to guide an American couple in Kyoto. He called their room from the lobby of their hotel, and they agreed to meet in 10 minutes.

An hour passed, but the Americans didn't show up. Just when the guide was about to give up and leave, an extremely angry American man and his wife entered the
5 hotel from the street, and when the guide asked them if they were his customers, the husband angrily accused him of being an hour late. The guide, ①taken aback, said that he had been on time and had been waiting for them at the agreed place, which angered the American even more. The American loudly insisted that the Japanese was lying, and that he and his wife had been waiting for an hour and knew that the
10 Japanese was late. Finally, puzzled by the American's angry insistence （　a　） what was clearly untrue（since the Japanese had been there since before the agreed time）, but ②anxious to soothe things over, the Japanese apologized by saying he was sorry. The American stopped shouting, but said to his wife, "You see, he admits he was lying!" The Japanese patiently ignored this, and guided the American couple as they
15 had requested. When they returned to the hotel, the lobby was full （　b　） other American members of the couple's tour group. The husband immediately began to tell the others,（　c　） a loud voice, how his guide had turned up an hour late and then had tried to ③lie his way out of it. In a final effort to soothe the American and allow them to part on friendly terms, the Japanese guide asked him for his US address so
20 that he could send him a Christmas card, as was his custom with foreigners he had guided.

This, however, enraged the American even more, and he loudly accused the Japanese, in front of all the other Americans, of trying to flatter him into paying （　d　） an extra hour by an insincere show of friendship.

25 Years later, the Japanese discovered that the root of the problem lay in English usage —— when he had said "at the front," he had meant "at the front desk," as it is used in Japanese English. But the American assumed he meant "at the front of the building," as it is used in standard English. So both had been "on time" at the "right place" —— ④neither had been lying.

30 From the American view point, the Japanese should not have apologized if he thought he was right. If he had argued back and refused to apologize, eventually （ideally）the truth would have emerged, and the misunderstanding would have been resolved.

［大妻女子大］

(1) (a)〜(d)に入る前置詞を下から選び，記号で答えよ。(2 点× 4)

ア at 　　　　**イ** for 　　　　**ウ** in 　　　　**エ** of
オ on 　　　　**カ** under 　　　**キ** over

(a) ⬚　　　(b) ⬚　　　(c) ⬚　　　(d) ⬚

(2) 下線部①と③の言い換えとして最も適当なものを 1 つずつ選び，記号で答えよ。(4 点× 2)

① taken aback

　ア at a loss 　　　　　　　**イ** for pleasure

　ウ in amazement 　　　　　**エ** with anger

③ lie his way out of it

　ア apologize for his laziness

　イ falsely escape from his responsibility

　ウ make a poor excuse for his lie

　エ steal out of the hotel

☆ (3) 下線部②と④を日本語に訳せ。(4 点× 2)

② anxious to soothe things over

④ neither had been lying

② 　　　　　　　　　　　　　　　　　　　　　　　　　　　　

④ 　　　　　　　　　　　　　　　　　　　　　　　　　　　　

(4) 日本人ガイドとアメリカ人観光客は，"at the front" をそれぞれどのように理解したか。両者の受け取り方の違いを簡潔に記せ。(6 点)

　　　　　　　　　　　　　　　　　　　　　　　　　　　　　　

━ notes ━

3. show up「現れる」　6. accuse O of 〜「O を〜という理由で非難する」
12. soothe「〜をなだめる」　apologize「謝る」　22. enrage「〜を怒らせる」
23. flatter O into *do*ing「O にこびて[をおだてて]〜させる」　27. assume「〜と思い込む」

41

　　The revolutions of the last two centuries have been so swift and radical that they have changed the most fundamental characteristic of the social order. Traditionally, the social order was hard and rigid. "Order" implied ☐(a)☐ and ☐(b)☐. Swift social revolutions were exceptional, and most social transformations resulted from the
5　accumulation of numerous small steps. Humans tended to assume that the social structure was inflexible and eternal. Families and communities might struggle to change their place within the order, but the idea that you could change the fundamental structure of the order was alien. People tended to reconcile themselves to existing conditions, declaring, "This is how it always was, and this is how it always will be."

10　　Over the last two centuries, the pace of change became so quick that the social order acquired a dynamic and flexible nature. It now exists in a state of permanent flow. When we speak of modern revolutions we tend to think of 1789 (the French Revolution) or 1917 (the Russian Revolution). But the fact is that, these days, every year is revolutionary. Today, even a thirty-year-old can honestly tell disbelieving
15　teenagers, "When I was young, the world was completely different." For example, the Internet came into wide usage from 1995 to 2000, but that was just about twenty years ago. Today we cannot imagine the world without it.

　　Hence any attempt to define the characteristics of modern society is similar ☐A☐ defining the color of a chameleon. The only characteristic of which we can be certain
20　is the ☐B☐. People have become used to this, and most of us think about the social order as something flexible, which we can engineer and improve at ☐C☐. The main promise of earlier rulers was to safeguard the traditional order or even go back to some lost golden age. In the last two centuries, the basis of politics has been that it promises to destroy the old world and build a better one in its place. Not even
25　the most conservative of political parties vows merely to keep things as they are. Everybody promises social reform, educational reform, economic reform — and they often fulfill those promises.

　　Just as scientists expect that the earth's movements will result in earthquakes and volcanic eruptions, so might we expect that drastic social movements will result in
30　bloody outbursts of violence. The political history of the nineteenth and twentieth centuries is often told as a series of deadly wars and revolutions. There is much truth here, but this all too familiar list of disasters is somewhat misleading. The modern age has seen uncommon levels not only of violence and horror, but also of peace and quietness.

（注）chameleon「カメレオン科のトカゲの総称」

［法政大-改］

(1) 空所 [(a)], [(b)] に入る最も適切な語の組み合わせを，つぎの**ア**〜**エ**の中から１つ選べ。(4点)

ア (a) anxiety　(b) change　　**イ** (a) stability　(b) continuity

ウ (a) patience　(b) conviction　**エ** (a) success　(b) failure

(2) 空所 [A] 〜 [C] に入る最も適切な語(句)を，それぞれ**ア**〜**エ**の中から１つ選べ。(3点×3)

[A]　**ア** at　　**イ** for　　**ウ** of　　**エ** to

[B]　**ア** constant change　　**イ** endless war
　　　　ウ permanent peace　　**エ** rigid order

[C]　**ア** all　　**イ** best　　**ウ** home　　**エ** will

(3) 下線部 Not even the most conservative of political parties vows merely to keep things as they are. の趣旨として最も適切なものを，つぎの**ア**〜**エ**の中から１つ選べ。(5点)

ア 現状の変更を公約に入れない政党が，最も保守的な政党とは限らない。

イ 最も保守的な政党でも，現状の維持だけを公約に掲げることはない。

ウ 最も保守的な政党でなければ，現状の変更を公約には入れない。

エ 現状の維持を公約に入れる政党は，最も保守的な政党だけである。

☆ (4) 本文の内容に合致するものをつぎの**ア**〜**カ**の中から１つ選べ。(6点)

ア People in the twenty-first century feel uneasy and uncomfortable because they know that they haven't kept up with the quick and drastic changes in society.

イ The French Revolution is usually regarded as a typical example of modern revolutions, but we should pay more attention to the Russian Revolution in terms of influence.

ウ It is quite difficult to identify major aspects of modern society, because it is moving too fast, and we tend to think that we can change the social order easily.

エ We don't understand how peaceful a life we are living, since economic, social and political changes have brought us the most peaceful era in human history.

オ Many political parties declare themselves to be reformists, but they are actually reluctant to make radical changes.

カ Emphasis on violence and horror in human history can give rise to a correct understanding of the world peace we are trying to achieve.

■ notes

1. swift「速やかな」　radical「過激な」　3. rigid「確固とした」　4. exceptional「例外的な」
5. accumulation「積み重ね」　8. alien「無縁の」　reconcile「〜を甘んじさせる」　18. hence「それゆえ」
22. safeguard「〜を守る」　25. conservative「保守的な」　vow「〜を公約する」
27. fulfill「(義務などを)果たす」　29. volcanic eruption「火山噴火」　drastic「過激な」
31. deadly「恐るべき」　32. misleading「誤解させる」

Water covers about 70% of the Earth's surface, and is the most common liquid. (a)Without water, there would be no life on the planet. Indeed, the earliest forms of life originated in the seas, and it was millions of years before primitive species began to emerge onto dry land.

5　Humans and other animals have bodies which are largely composed of fluid, and, apart from a few species which get their liquid from food, they need to drink water regularly to maintain a healthy balance. Humans can live for weeks without food, but ①only a matter of days without water.

Water is also necessary for our food supply; many people depend on fish as a major
10　food but, more importantly, plants, which are at the base of all food chains, need water to germinate, to photosynthesise and to grow.

Unfortunately, in many areas of the world, water is in short supply, or is poorly managed. Shortage of water means plants and ②livestock cannot thrive. People become malnourished, and may die, either directly from thirst, or through lack of
15　resistance to disease. In recent years, rainfall seems to have become more unreliable, and deserts are spreading. ③How much of this is due to human activity is a matter for debate, but some of it certainly is. Even in countries such as Britain, where there is fairly plentiful rainfall, fresh water can run low because of the enormous demands from domestic users, industry and agriculture.

20　For people and animals to thrive, they need not just adequate water, but clean water. Many organisms thrive in water, including some which are harmful to human life, like the cholera bacterium. Drinking water also needs to be free of poisonous mineral and chemical pollutants.

④But water is more than just a matter of survival. We rely on it to clean ourselves
25　and our possessions; we use it as a means of transport and as a source of energy for our mills and hydroelectric power stations; ⑤in industry it serves as a coolant and as a solvent; we extract vital minerals from it; and we often find ourselves spiritually refreshed just by looking at it and listening to it. It is such an integral part of our lives that it is a major symbol in many religions and often has a ritual significance.

30　Sadly, we also treat water as the world's rubbish bin —— a convenient dumping ground for all kinds of waste, from human body wastes to radioactive material. Many other pollutants end up in our rivers, lakes and oceans accidentally. (b)We are in danger of making life impossible for vast numbers of different species which live in the water, and of poisoning the water supplies on which our very lives depend.

（注）photosynthesise「光合成する」 radioactive「放射性の」

[東京女子大]

☆ (1) 下線部(a)，(b)を日本語に直せ。(6点×2)

(a)	
(b)	

(2) 下線部②，③の内容に合うものをア〜オから選べ。(②4点，③6点)

② ア animals　　イ animals and humans
　ウ animals kept by farmers　　エ people　　オ trees

③ ア It is not clear to what extent the increasing unreliability of rainfall and the spreading of deserts are caused by human beings.
　イ The increasing unreliability of rainfall is clearly caused by human beings.
　ウ The increasing unreliability of rainfall and the spreading of deserts are clearly caused by human beings.
　エ The spreading of deserts may or may not be caused by human beings.
　オ We should discuss whether or not the increasing unreliability of rainfall and the spreading of deserts are caused by human beings.

(3) 下線部①，④，⑤とそれぞれほぼ同じ内容にするには＿＿にどのような英単語を入れればよいかを答えよ。(4点×3)

① Humans ＿＿＿＿ only ＿＿＿＿ a few days without water.
④ But we do not need water only ＿＿＿＿ ＿＿＿＿.
⑤ In industry it ＿＿＿＿ ＿＿＿＿ as a coolant and as a solvent.

①	

④	

⑤	

■ notes
4. emerge「現れる」　5. fluid「水分，液体」　10. food chain「食物連鎖」　11. germinate「発芽する」
13. thrive「成長する」　14. malnourished「栄養失調の」　21. organism「有機体，生物」
22. mineral「ミネラル，無機物」　27. extract「〜を抽出する」　vital「重要な」　28. integral「不可欠の」
29. ritual「儀式の」　30. rubbish bin「ごみ箱」

When members of a group are working cooperatively, they can clearly accomplish more than a single individual can.　Indeed, some human achievements are possible only when several people participate through a group process that (a)integrates their contributions.　The economic, technological, and political complexity of contemporary
5　society demands such diverse skills that no one can ever hope to master them all. Most industrial, scientific, and governmental enterprises now require many specialists, each contributing expertise in a different field.

However, researchers studying group processes have discovered that as groups increase in size, each group member's contribution tends to (b)decline.　In the late
10　1920's, researchers found that when people pull together on a rope, each exerts less force than if he or she were pulling on the rope alone.　Working alone, one person pulled nearly 63 kg, but two people working together pulled, not 126 kg (2 × 63), but 118 kg.　And three people pulled 160 kg, which is only about two and one half times what a single individual pulls.　This and other studies led to the conclusion that people
15　work less hard when they are part of a group than when they work alone.　Apparently, individuals slacken their efforts when there are many contributors to a common task. In short, they become lazy.

The social impact theory holds that the larger the group, the less pressure there is on any one member to produce.　The theory suggests that it is the diffusion of
20　responsibility for the group's work that leads each individual to reduce his or her effort. Social psychologist Stephen Harkins suggested in the late 1980's that it is specifically the anonymity of performance that encourages laziness.　When each individual believes that no one can (c)detect how much he or she is contributing, all tend to produce less. When individual contributions can be identified, as when the experimenter measures
25　how much each has contributed, laziness is reduced.

Researchers have discovered that being evaluated by others is not the only thing that keeps people working.　When people can evaluate their own performance by comparing it to the previous performance of others on the same task, they work hard —— even though the experimenter cannot (d)calculate how much they have contributed.
30　Self-evaluation apparently provides them with the satisfaction of matching or surpassing the "standard" performance on the task.　It seems that ①social laziness develops when there is no way for people to tell how well they are doing.

（注）expertise：expert knowledge

［関西学院大-改］

■ notes

5. diverse「多様な」　6. enterprise「事業」　10. exert「(力などを)働かせる」
16. slacken「(仕事などを)怠ける」　19. diffusion「拡散，分散」　21. specifically「厳密に言えば」
22. anonymity「匿名(性)」　26. evaluate「～を評価する」　30. surpass「～より優れている」

(1) 下線部(a)〜(d)の意味に最も近いものをそれぞれア〜エから選べ。(2点×4)

    (a) integrates

    ア combines   **イ** commands   **ウ** contests   **エ** forsakes

    (b) decline

    ア encourage   **イ** enlarge   **ウ** diminish   **エ** refuse

    (c) detect

    ア contain   **イ** perceive   **ウ** praise   **エ** trust

    (d) calculate

    ア split   **イ** speculate   **ウ** measure   **エ** appreciate

☆ (2) 下線部①を日本語に訳せ。(6点)

☆ (3) 次の英文の中から，本文の内容と一致するものを４つ選べ。(6点×4)

    ア It is the complexity and specialty of tasks in our contemporary world that bar expert and individual contribution in cooperative group projects.

    イ Group process researchers have found that generally, the larger a group is, the smaller the contribution of its individual members will be.

    ウ Contemporary society has provided so much convenience and so many special services that we no longer have to do such simple tasks as pulling a rope to transport goods.

    エ Researchers have found that the pulling force of a group of subjects using a rope in an experiment is not exactly a multiple of the number of group members.

    オ Studies in social psychology have revealed that social laziness is promoted when an individual's contribution in a group task is not easily identified.

    カ Researchers have found that competitive and special-skill work encourages higher performance of individual group members than cooperative and general-skill tasks.

    キ According to recent research findings, both self-and outside-evaluations of individual work encourage more efforts on the part of group members than otherwise.

Foreign language instruction should come early in the educational process, basically at the elementary level. This is because it can serve as a fundamental shaper of the child's perception of the world. It can help him accept the fact that there is much in the world that differs greatly from what he sees around him and to which he must learn

5　to accommodate himself. It should come early also because the young child learns a foreign language with ease and pleasure. At that stage it can be one of the really fun elements in education, not the meaningless drudgery it has seemed to generations of students who took (a)it up later in their schooling.

　　The modern, more efficient techniques of language teaching through native

10　speakers and electronic audio-visual aids also are particularly effective with young children. At (b)that age it is natural for them to learn a foreign language through imitation and repetition, as they did with their native language. The older they become, the more resistant (c)they are to this process and the more dependent on a rational effort to substitute the foreign language, element by element, for (d)the patterns of

15　language already established in their minds, becoming in the process grammarians more than speakers.

　　The question of which languages should be studied is probably less important than when they should be studied. One criterion in the selection of a foreign language would be foreseeable utility in later life. From this point of view, Spanish, French,

20　German, and Italian would seem natural favorites for Americans. Another criterion would be differentness from English. The greater the difference, the more value will be derived from the experience, both in terms of understanding the diversity of the world and in realizing the logical limitations of any language. An overlapping of the practical utility and difference factors would point toward such important but very

25　different languages as Japanese, Chinese, Arabic, Hindi, Swahili, and Russian.

　　Foreign language study, I realize, is at present an unpopular cause. (e)It is regarded as unstimulating rote memory work of little relevance for most young people. These criticisms do have considerable validity when leveled at the conception and practice of much foreign language instruction in (f)our schools today. But (g)if properly understood

30　and implemented, the teaching of foreign languages could be a key element in preparing the next generation for successful membership in the emerging world community.

[明星大]

☆ (1) 第1段落の内容を最もよく言い当てているのはどれか。記号で答えよ。(4点)

    ア 外国語の学習は自己を相対化するために必要である。

    イ 子どもは外国語の習得が早い。

    ウ 外国語教育は教育の初期段階でやるべきだ。

(2) 次の問いに答えよ。(4点×3)

    ① 下線部(a)の it は何を指すか。文中の英語で答えよ。

    ② 下線部(c)の they は何を指すか。文中の英語で答えよ。

    ③ 下線部(e)の It は何を指すか。文中の英語で答えよ。

(3) 下線(b)の that age は次のどれが最も適当か。記号で答えよ。(4点)

    ア 3歳ごろ   **イ** 8歳ごろ   **ウ** 13歳ごろ   **エ** 18歳ごろ

(4) 下線(f)の our schools とはどこの国の学校のことか,日本語で答えよ。また,それが分かるのは何番目の段落の何番目のセンテンスかを数字で答えよ。(6点)

(5) 下線部(g)の部分は省略文であるが,その省略された主語は何か。本文中にそれを見出して,1語も省くことなく英語で答えよ。(6点)

☆ (6) 下線部(d)の部分を日本語にせよ。(4点)

■ notes

2. shaper「形成するもの」 5. accommodate *oneself* to ～「～に適応する」
7. meaningless drudgery「無意味な骨折り仕事」 13. rational「合理的な」
14. substitute「～を置き換える」 18. criterion「基準」 19. utility「実用性」 22. diversity「多様性」
24. point toward ～「～を示す」 27. rote「機械的な記憶」 of little relevance「ほとんど関連性のない」
28. validity「正当さ,妥当性」

Some new technologies are frightening from the start and create an instant consensus on the need to establish political controls over their development and use. When the first atomic bomb exploded at Alamogordo, New Mexico, in the summer of 1945, ①not one of the witnesses to the event failed to understand that a terrible new
5 potential for destruction had been created. Nuclear weapons were thus from the start ringed with ②political controls: individuals could not freely develop nuclear technology on their own or traffic in the parts necessary to create atomic bombs, and, in time, nations that signed to the 1968 Non-Proliferation Treaty agreed to control international trade in nuclear technology.

10 Other new technologies appear to be much more harmless, and consequently subject to little or no regulation. Personal computers and the Internet are examples: these new forms of information technology (IT) promised to create wealth, spread access to information and therefore power around more democratically, and foster community among their users. People had to look hard for negative impacts from the Information
15 Revolution; what they have found to date are issues like the so-called digital divide (that is, inequality of access of IT) and threats to privacy, neither of which qualify as earth-shaking matters of justice or morality. Despite occasional efforts on the part of the world's more statist societies to try to control the use of IT, it has blossomed in recent years with minimal regulatory oversight on either a national or international level.

20 Biotechnology falls somewhere between ③these extremes. Transgenic crops and human genetic engineering make people far more uneasy than do personal computers and the Internet. But biotechnology also promises important benefits for human health and well-being. When presented with an advance like the ability to cure a child of cystic fibrosis or diabetes, people find it difficult to articulate reasons why their
25 unease with the technology should ④stand in the way of progress. It is easiest to object to a new biotechnology if its development leads to an unsuccessful clinical trial or to a deadly allergic reaction to a genetically modified food. But the real threat of biotechnology is far more subtle, and therefore harder to weigh in practical terms.

In the face of the challenge from a technology like this, where good and bad are
30 intimately connected, it seems to me that there can be only one possible response: countries must regulate the development and use of technology politically, setting up institutions that will discriminate between those technological advances that promote human flourishing, and those that pose a threat to human dignity and well-being. These regulatory institutions must first be empowered to enforce ⑤these discrimina-
35 tions on a national level, and must ultimately extend their reach internationally.

(Adapted from *Our Posthuman Future* by Francis Fukuyama)

（注）Non-Proliferation Treaty「核不拡散条約」　statist societies「政治的な権力や影響力が強い社会」
transgenic crops「遺伝子組換作物」　cystic fibrosis「囊胞性線維症（遺伝性疾患の一種）」　diabetes「糖尿病」

［藤女子大-改］

☆ (1) 下線部①を和訳せよ。(6点)

(2) 下線部②の内容として本文中で説明されているものをア～エから1つ選べ。(5点)

　　ア 核兵器の輸送に必要な道路整備をすることへの政治的規制

　　イ 原子爆弾を製造するために必要な情報を集めることへの政治的規制

　　ウ 個人が勝手に核開発にかかわることへの政治的規制

　　エ 自国の利益のために核兵器を利用することへの政治的規制

(3) 下線部③は具体的に何を表しているか。その組み合わせとして最も適当なものをア～カから1つ選べ。

(4点)

　　ア biotechnology／information technology　　イ biotechnology／genetic technology

　　ウ biotechnology／nuclear technology　　エ genetic technology／information technology

　　オ genetic technology／nuclear technology

　　カ information technology／nuclear technology

(4) 下線部④の意味に最も近いものをア～エから選べ。(4点)

　　ア facilitate　　イ interrupt　　ウ maintain　　エ make

(5) 下線部⑤の内容をまとめると下記のようになる。空所（　A　）と（　B　）に入る日本語を書け。(A
　　とBは順不同)

(5点×2)

　　（　A　）と（　B　）を区別すること

A	
B	

■ notes

2. consensus「合意形成」　6. ring「～を包囲する」　7. traffic in ～「～を不正に売買する」
10. consequently「結果的に」　13. foster「～を発展させる」　16. earth-shaking「きわめて重大な」
19. minimal「最低限の」　regulatory oversight「規制管理」　21. genetic engineering「遺伝子工学」
23. well-being「幸福」　24. articulate「～をはっきり述べる」　26. clinical trial「臨床試験」
27. allergic reaction「アレルギー反応」　28. subtle「微妙な」　30. intimately「密接に」
32. discriminate「～を見分ける」　33. flourish「繁栄する」　pose「～をもたらす」　dignity「尊厳」
34. empower「～に権限を与える」　35. ultimately「最終的に」

I must have been seventeen or eighteen when I worked one summer in a hotel run by my aunt. I don't know how much I got — twenty-two dollars a month, I think — and I alternated eleven hours one day and thirteen the next as a desk clerk or as a busboy in the restaurant. And during the afternoon, when you were a desk clerk, you
5 had to bring milk up to Mrs. D —, an invalid woman who never gave you a tip. That's the way the world was: You worked long hours and got nothing for it, every day.

This was a resort hotel, by the beach, on the outskirts of New York City. The husbands would go to work in the city and leave the wives behind to play cards, so you would always have to get the bridge tables out. Then at night the guys would play
10 poker, so you'd get the tables ready for them — clean out the ashtrays and so on. I was always up until late at night, like two o'clock, so it really *was* thirteen and eleven hours a day.

There were certain things I didn't like, such as tipping. (a)I thought we should be paid more, and not have to have any tips. But when I proposed that to the boss, I got
15 nothing but laughter. She told everybody, "Richard doesn't want his tips, hee, hee; he doesn't want his tips, ha, ha, ha." The world is full of this kind of dumb smart-alec who doesn't understand anything.

Anyway, at one stage there was a group of men who, when they'd come back from working in the city, would ①right away want ice for their drinks. Now the other guy
20 working with me had really been a desk clerk. He was older than I was, and a lot more professional. One time he said to me, "Listen, we're always bringing ice up to that guy Ungar and he never gives us a tip — not even ten cents. Next time, when they ask for ice, just don't do a damn thing. Then they'll call you back, and when they call you back, you say, 'Oh, I'm sorry. I forgot. We're all forgetful sometimes.' "

25 So ②I did it, and Ungar gave me fifteen cents! But now, when I think back on it, I realize that the other desk clerk, the professional, had *really* known what to do — tell the other guy to ③take the risk of getting into trouble. He put *me* to the job of training this fellow to give tips. *He* never said anything; he made *me* do it!

I had to clean up tables in the dining room as a busboy. You pile all this stuff from the tables on to a tray at the side, and when it gets high enough you carry it into the kitchen. So you get a new tray, right? You *should* do it in two steps — take the old tray away, and put in a new one — but I thought, "I'm going to do it in one step." So I tried to slide the new tray under, and pull the old tray out at the same time, and it slipped — BANG! All the stuff went on the floor. And then, naturally, the question was, "What were you doing? How did it fall?" Well, how could I explain that I was trying to invent a new way to handle trays?

Among the desserts there was some kind of coffee cake that came out very pretty on a doily, on a little plate. But if you would go in the back you'd see a man called the pantryman. His problem was to get the stuff ready for desserts. Now this man must have been a miner, or something — heavy-built, with very short, rounded, thick fingers. He'd take this stack of doilies, which are manufactured by some sort of stamping process, all stuck together, and (b)with these fingers he'd try to separate the doilies to put them on the plates. I always heard him say, ④"Damn these doilies!" while he was doing this, and I remember thinking, "What a contrast — the person sitting at the table gets this nice cake on a doilied plate, while the pantryman back there with the short and thick thumbs is saying, 'Damn these doilies!' " So that was the difference between the real world and ⑤what it looked like.

(注)busboy「食堂給仕人の助手」　smart-alec「利口ぶった人」
　　doily「(皿の上に敷いてサンドイッチやケーキなどを置く紙やリネンで作った小さな)敷物」
　　pantryman「配膳室係」
　　　　　　はいぜん
　　　[立命館大]

■ notes
3. alternate「～を交互に行う」　5. invalid「病弱な」　7. outskirts「郊外」
10. ashtray「灰皿」　21. professional「本職の，ベテランの」　23. call back「～を呼び戻す」
27. get into trouble「トラブルになる」　train「～を訓練する，～に教え込む」
37. dessert「デザート」　38. back「奥，裏手」　40. miner「炭鉱労働者」
heavy-built「体格のがっちりした」　41. stack「積み重ねたもの，束」
42. stamping process「プレス加工(＝型を押しつけるような工程)」
stuck stick(くっつく)の過去分詞形　44. contrast「際立った違い」　46. thumb「親指」

☆ (1) 下線部(a), (b)を和訳せよ。(4点× 2)

(a)	
(b)	

(2) 下線部①〜⑤の意味・内容または説明として最も近いものをア〜エから１つずつ選び，その記号を書け。(4点× 5)

① right away

　ア very much

　イ without any delay

　ウ naturally

　エ all the way

② I did it

　ア I called them back for a tip

　イ I followed the advice of the desk clerk

　ウ I forgot to bring ice up to Ungar

　エ I did what they asked me to do

③ take the risk of getting into trouble

　ア take care to keep out of trouble

　イ avoid the possibility of having problems

　ウ start serious trouble

　エ face the danger of running into trouble

④ "Damn these doilies!"

  ア an expression of impatience

  イ an expression of satisfaction

  ウ an expression of disappointment

  エ an expression of sorrow

⑤ what it looked like

  ア that this man must have been a miner, or something

  イ "Damn these doilies!"

  ウ that the person sitting at the table gets this nice cake on a doilied plate

  エ that the pantryman back there with the short and thick thumbs is saying, "Damn these doilies!"

☆ (3) 本文の内容と一致するものをア～カから２つ選び, その番号を答えよ。（３つ以上答えてはならない。）

（6点×2）

  ア My working hours varied from day to day at my uncle's hotel.

  イ Working long hours meant that I would receive a reward for it.

  ウ The resort hotel was located on the edge of New York City, where the husbands would go to work from the hotel during the day, leaving their wives behind.

  エ The boss laughed at me when I complained to her that I had received no tip from the invalid woman.

  オ Though I thought it was a good idea to replace the old tray with a new one at one and the same time, I couldn't succeed in doing it.

  カ A heavy-built pantryman in the hotel taught me what went on in the world by telling me about his life.

装丁デザイン　ブックデザイン研究所
本文デザイン　A.S.T DESIGN
編集協力　　　エディット

大学入試 ステップアップ 英語長文【標準】

編 著 者	大学入試問題研究会		発 行 所	受験研究社
発 行 者	岡 本 泰 治			
印 刷 所	ユ ニ ッ ク ス		© 株式会社 増進堂・受験研究社	

〒550-0013 大阪市西区新町2丁目19番15号

注文・不良品などについて：(06)6532-1581(代表)／本の内容について：(06)6532-1586(編集)

注意 本書を無断で複写・複製（電子化を含む）
して使用すると著作権法違反となります。

Printed in Japan　高廣製本
落丁・乱丁本はお取り替えします。

大学入試 ステップ アップ
STEP UP↗

Standard
標準

英語長文

解答・解説

01 小さなアメフト選手　(pp. 4〜5)

```
(1)  (A)エ   (B)オ   (C)ア   (D)ウ
(2)  (a)ア   (b)イ   (c)エ   (d)ウ
(3)  ウ
(4)  全文訳 の下線部参照。
```

解説

(1)(A) at the same time「同時に」
(B) provide A with B「A に B を供給する」
(C) slip into 〜「〜にそっと入る」
(D) feel sorry for 〜「〜を気の毒に思う」

(2)(a) enroll「〜を登録する」　(b) mumble「(聞き取りにくい声で)つぶやく」　(c) give in「譲歩する」
(d) before long「まもなく」

(3)「決勝のタッチダウンを決めた」「大喜びで彼を担ぎ上げた」といった前後の内容から推測する。break loose「(歓声などが)どっと沸く」(= erupt)

(4)生きている間父親は盲目だったが、天国に行けば見ることができるようになるはずだと信じて、このように言った。

全文訳

心の底からアメリカンフットボールを愛している、やせた若い少年がいた。練習のたびに、彼は熱心に持てる力を出し切った。しかし、身体の大きさがほかの少年たちの半分しかなかったので、いい結果をまったく出せなかった。この希望に満ちた選手は、すべての試合でベンチに座るのみで、めったにプレーしなかった。この 10 代の若者は、父親と 2 人暮らしだった。息子はいつもベンチにいるだけだったが、父親はいつもスタンドで応援していた。

その若者は大学に進学したとき、フットボールチームに入ろうと決めた。だれもが、彼はメンバーにはなれないだろうと確信していた。しかし、監督は彼をメンバーに入れた。彼がいつも練習に熱心に取り組んで、ほかのメンバーにぜひとも必要な気迫や闘争心をもたらすからだ。

彼の 4 年生のフットボールシーズンも終わろうという頃、大事なプレーオフの試合の直前に彼が練習場に走り出たとき、監督は 1 通の電報を手にして彼を呼んだ。その若者は電報を読み、死んだように黙り込んだ。泣きたい気持ちをぐっとこらえて、彼は小声で監督に言った。「今朝、父が亡くなりました。今日は練習を休んでもいいですか」

監督は、彼の肩を優しく抱いて言った。「今週いっぱい休みなさい。土曜日の試合のために戻ってこようなどと考えるなよ」

土曜日になり、試合は劣勢だった。第 3 クォーター、チームが 10 点差で負けていたとき、無口な若者がだれもいないロッカールームにそっと入り、プロテクターを身に着け

た。彼が走ってサイドラインに現れると、監督や選手たちは熱心なチームメイトがこんなにも早く戻ってきたのを見て驚いた。

「監督、僕にプレーさせてください。今日はどうしてもプレーしなければならないんです」と、その若者は言った。

監督は、聞こえないふりをした。彼は、接戦になっているプレーオフの試合に、いちばん下手な選手を出したくはなかった。しかし、その若者がしつこく食い下がると、その若者に同情した監督はついに折れた。「よし」彼は言った。「行っていいぞ」

ほどなくして、監督、選手たち、そしてスタンドの全員が目を疑った。それまでプレーしたことのなかった、この小さな無名選手が完ぺきなプレーをしていたのだ。相手チームは彼を止めることができなかった。彼はスター選手のように走り、パスし、ブロックし、タックルした。チームは点差を縮め始めた。まもなく、同点になった。残り時間数秒のところで、その若者は長い距離を走り、決勝のタッチダウンを決めた。ファンは狂喜乱舞した。チームメイトたちは大喜びで彼を担ぎ上げた。

スタンドが空になり、チームの選手たちがシャワーを浴び、ロッカールームを出て行ったあと、監督は、この若者がひとり隅っこで静かに座っているのに気づいた。監督は彼のところに来て言った。「信じられない。すばらしかった！　何があったのか教えてくれ。どうやったんだ？」

彼は監督を見て、目に涙を浮かべながら言った。「父が亡くなったのはご存じですね。ですが、父が盲目だったことはご存じでしたか」その若者は涙をこらえて笑顔を作った。「父は、全試合に来てくれました。でも、今日初めて、僕がプレーする姿を見ることができたのです。僕だって活躍できるんだと見せてあげたかったのです！」

Point

過去完了

① This little unknown, who had never played before, was doing everything right.
(それまでプレーしたことのなかった、この小さな無名選手が完ぺきにプレーしていたのだ。)

② After the team had left the locker room, the coach noticed that this young man was sitting quietly all alone.
(チームの選手たちがロッカールームを出て行ったあと、監督は、この若者がひとりで静かに座っているのに気づいた。)

解説

過去完了は、過去のある時点を基準として、その時点までの完了・結果・経験・継続を表す。

①では，試合に出てプレーしていたときが基準で，その時点までの**経験**（「(試合に出て)プレーしたことがなかった」）を表している。

②では，監督が気づいたときが基準で，その時までにほかの選手たちがロッカールームを去っていたこと（**完了**。「去った結果，もうそこにはいない」という意味で**結果**と取ることもできる）を表している。

現在を基準とするか，過去のある時点を基準とするかの違いがあるが，考え方は現在完了と同じ。現在完了については，「人間の役に立つ昆虫」の Point を参照。(p.5)

02 インターネットと頭の働き （pp.6〜7）

(1) ①ア ②ウ ③ア ④エ ⑤ウ
(2) 全文訳 の下線部参照。

解説

(1)①「筆者はなぜ長いテキストを読んでいると気が散ってくるのか」 **ア**「彼がインターネットの情報を拾い読みすることに慣れてしまったから」 ②「筆者の言う下線部(a)の『高くつく』とはどういう意味か」 **ウ**「インターネットのせいで私たちは深く考える力を失いつつある」 cost O_1 O_2 で「(主語によって)O_1 が O_2 を失う」という意味。 ③「若者を対象にした調査から主にわかったことは何か」 **ア**「若者の情報の取り入れ方が変わった」 ④「本文によると，次のうちのどれが『リニアな』頭を最も適切に説明しているか」 **エ**「長く難しい文に集中し続ける力」 ⑤「筆者はインターネットをどう思っているか」 **ウ**「私たちから大切で特別な何かを奪いつつある」 rob A of B で「A から B を奪う」。

(2) whether 〜 or not「〜かどうかに関係なく」 expect to *do*「〜することを期待する」 take in 〜「〜を取り込む」 the way は接続詞のような働きをして，the way S V で「S が V する(のと同じ)ように」という意味になる。

全文訳 どうやら頭がおかしくなったらしい。この何年かずっと，だれかが，あるいは何かが，私の脳の働きに手を加えているような違和感がある。完全に頭がおかしくなったわけではないが，脳の働きが変わっているのはわかる。何かを読んでいるときに，いちばん強く感じる。以前は，1冊の本や長い記事に夢中になるなんて，わけもないことだった。それがもうほぼありえない。今では，私の集中力は1，2ページもすると，あてもなくふわふわと漂いだす。ちょっと読んだら，何かほかにすることを求め始めているのだ。怠け癖のある脳を文面に引き戻してばかりいるような気がする。

何が起きているのかは理解しているつもりだ。10年以上もの間，インターネットで検索したりネットサーフィンをしたりして，多くの時間をオンラインで過ごしている。私はライターだから，インターネットは調べ物をするのに多くの時間を短縮してくれる。コンピュータを使って支払いをしたり，アポを取ったり，フライトやホテルの部屋を予約したり，ほかにもいろんなことをしたりする。仕事をしていないときでも，メールを読んだり書いたり，記事の見出しに目を走らせたり，Instagram にざっと目を通したり，YouTube で短い動画を見たり，リンクからリンクに移動したり。

こうしたことはすべて，仕事にとっても遊びにとっても恩恵がある。情報へのアクセスが本当に簡単だ！ ただし，こうした恩恵は代償を強いられる。インターネットは単なる情報チャンネルというわけではない。私たちの思考プロセスを形作るものでもある。しかも，インターネットがやっているように思えるのは，私の集中力や思考力を低下させることだ。ネットワークにつながっているかどうかに関係なく，今や私の頭は，インターネットが送りつけてくるのと同じように，つまり細かい情報パケットが目まぐるしく流れてくるように，情報を取り入れようと待ちかまえている。落ち着きのある，集中した私の意識は，一気に，何の脈絡もなく，次から次に大量に押し寄せる情報を取り入れたがる，新手の意識によって脇へ追いやられる——速いほどいいのだ。

以前，ある調査会社がインターネット利用の若者への影響に関する調査報告を発表した。同社はインターネットを使いながら育った 6,000 人の子どもに聞き込みを行った。この会社は，インターネットが若者の情報の取り入れ方に影響を及ぼすと報告した。「子どもはページを必ずしも左から右に，上から下に読むわけではありません。そうではなく，飛ばし読みして，興味のある大事な情報にさっと目を通している可能性があります」

私たち人間はかつて「リニアな」頭を持っていた——集中力を失わずに，長くて難解なテキストを処理するのに長けた頭だ。ところが今や，それは変わりつつある。この 500 年の間，印刷機のおかげで書物を読むことが一般的な活動になって以来，リニアな頭は芸術，科学，社会の中心を担ってきた。今ではもう，そんな頭は過去のものなのかもしれない。

Point

the way S V の表現
①「S が V する方法」
I don't like **the way** he speaks to me.
（私に対する彼の口の利き方が気に食わない。）
②「S が V するように」
I wish I could dance **the way** I used to.
（昔のように踊れたらいいのに。）

解説

the way は，あとに S V を続けて接続詞のように使われることがある。①は，関係副詞 how の先行詞にあたる the way だけが how の代わりに

使われる形。「〜する方法 [様子]，〜のしかた」という意味で，like の目的語になっていることからわかるように名詞節のような働きをする。関係副詞 how を使って次のように書き換えることができる。

①＝ I don't like *how* he speaks to me.

②は「〜するように」という意味で，副詞節のような働きをする。例文では used to のあとの dance が省略されている。直訳すると「私がかつて踊ったように」という意味になる。様態を表す接続詞 as を使って次のように書き換えることができる。

②＝ I wish I could dance as I used to.

03 エクイトレード　　(pp. 8〜9)

(1)　(A)ウ　(B)イ　(C)エ　(D)ア
(2)　①エ　②ウ　③ア
(3)　全文訳 の下線部参照。
(4)　イ，エ

解説

(1)(A) for sale「販売されて」　(B) thanks to 〜「〜のおかげで」　(C) source of 〜「〜の出所，よりどころ」　(D) share A with B「A を B と共有する」

(2)① added value「付加価値」　mediocre「月並みな」　face value「額面」　low「低い」　② effect「効果，影響」　rumor「噂」　web site「ホームページ」　regulation「規制」　③ local market「地元市場」　high-end market「高級品市場」　fruit and vegetable market「青果市場」　international market「国際市場」

(3) aim to *do*「〜することを目的 [目標] とする」　finished goods「完成品」　raw material「原材料」

(4)ア「マダガスカルで生産されるチョコレートの 11 パーセントは地元で消費される」11 パーセントは，チョコレートバーの値段の内で，マダガスカルの政府が税金として受け取る比率。　イ「著者は，エクイトレードがフェアトレードよりもずっとよいと考えている」第 3 段落最終文 (*l.* 22) を参照。　ウ「著者が子どもの頃に訪れたチョコレート工場は，ロンドンにあった」マダガスカルのアンタナナリボにあった。　エ「専門知識の移転はマダガスカルの経済に大いに役立った」第 4 段落参照。

全文訳　私が 10 歳くらいの頃，その学年 1 年間でのいちばん大きな出来事は，マダガスカルのアンタナナリボにあるロバート・チョコレート工場への社会科見学だった。大きな白い部屋や倉庫に山ほどあるチョコレートの箱の記憶が昨日よみがえったのは，妻がその同じ工場で作られたチョコレートバーを私に差し出したときであった。それは現在，ロンドンにある有名な店で売られている。サンビラーノという異なったブランド名で売られているが，ちょっと

調べれば，それがロバート工場製であるというだけでなく，エクイトレードと呼ばれるすばらしい活動の成果であるということもわかる。

エクイトレードは，フェアトレードと似たものであるが，いくつかの重要な点で異なっている。フェアトレードとは結局のところ，農家を対象としたものであり，小規模の農家や生産者に公正（フェア）な価格を保証するものである。作物に対しては公正な価格が保証されるが，製品自体，したがって利益は，別の場所で生み出されることになる。エクイトレードは，原材料よりもむしろ，完成品の販売のサポートを目的としている。それには完成品に対する付加価値がついてくる。こうすることで，利益の大半はその発展途上国に留まり，税金は地元政府に支払われることになり，この取り引きによって，国全体が利益を享受できるのだ。

チョコレートバーの例を見てみよう。イギリスの新聞ガーディアンのジョン・ヴィダル記者によれば，フェアトレードのチョコレートバーの値段の平均はおよそ 2.20 ドルである。その内のほんのわずかしか，原料のカカオ豆が栽培された国には留まらず，あなたが支払う値段の 2 〜 3 パーセント程度である。チョコレート自体は別の場所で製造されるため，値段の残りの部分は先進国の製造業者，供給業者，小売業者などに行ってしまう。エクイトレードは，一連の生産工程全体が地元に留まるように機能するため，サンビラーノというチョコレートバーの小売価格の 51 パーセントがマダガスカルに留まる。このほうがずっとよいという意見に，あなたも賛同するはずだ。

エクイトレードに関連した影響はたくさんある。第 1 に，途上国への専門知識の移転がある。この事例では，起業家がイギリスのシェフやレストラン経営者の主要な団体である英国の料理芸術アカデミーと共同で，市場に出すチョコレートの準備をした。ロバート工場は何十年にもわたって，地元市場向けに菓子類の製造を続けていたが，現在では国際市場でも戦える，世界レベルの製品を生産している。この技術移転は，農家の人々に至るまですべての供給網に及び，農家の人々はイギリスからの技術支援のおかげで，よりよい方法を使って，より品質の高いカカオ豆を生産している。

第 2 に，ここマダガスカルに対する高い名声である。愛好家たちは昔から，マダガスカルのカカオ豆を賞賛してきたが，それがより広く認識されるのは悪いことではない。有名なアニメ映画と同じ名前を持つこの貧しい国にとって，単にサンビラーノの豆が栽培されているだけでなく，加工，箱詰めまでもがマダガスカル国内で行われていることは，本当に誇らしいことであるに違いない。マダガスカルの国際的な名声を確立することは，国の自信のためにもすばらしいことであるが，同時に，さらなる投資を呼び込むことにもなり，それはすなわち，さらなる発展や雇用を生み，経済成長にもつながる。エクイトレードが持つもうひとつの重要な要素が税金である。より多くのお金がマダガスカル国内に留まるので，政府はより多い分け前，この場合，チョコレートバーの値段の 11 パーセントを得る。このお金は国庫に入り，教育や医療，公共投資を可能にするのだ。

Point

SVOC

① Equitrade keeps the whole production chain local.

（エクイトレードでは，生産工程全体が地元に留まっている。）

② The money makes education, healthcare and public spending projects possible.

（そのお金で，教育や医療，公共投資が可能になる。）

解説

　　SVOC は，O（目的語）＝ C（補語）の関係が成り立つ文型。文法問題として出されれば理解できる人でも，長文の中に出てきた場合，慣れていないとなかなか気づきにくい場合がある。

　　① は，S ＝ Equitrade，V ＝ keeps，O ＝ the whole production，C ＝ local で，「生産工程全体」＝「地元の」という関係が成り立っている。

　　② は，S ＝ The money，V ＝ makes，O ＝ education, healthcare and public spending projects，C ＝ possible で，「教育や医療，公共投資」＝「可能な」という関係が成り立っている。

　　①②は，説明用に簡略化した文なので，実際の本文でどのように使われていたか，確認しておくように。

04 インド人の時間感覚　　(pp. 10〜11)

(1)　①ア　②ウ　③ア　④ア　⑤ウ
(2)　**全文訳** の下線部(a)，(b)参照。

解説

(1)①第 1 段落参照。**ア** be unaware of 〜「〜に気づかない」　②第 2 段落第 3 文(*ll.* 6-8)に「のんびりと (leisurely)仕事をしている」とある。　③第 3 段落第 3 文(*ll.* 15-16)に Finally I managed to find my way to his place とある。**ア** succeed in *do*ing「〜することに成功する」　④第 3 段落第 3 文(*ll.* 15-16)後半 only to 以下に「電報はまだ配達されていなかった」とある。**ア** as expected「思っていたように」　⑤最終段落の内容から考える。とくに，最終文(*l.* 23) の What a big contrast on this same earth! に着目する。

(2)(a) attend to 〜「〜に従事する」 duty「義務→しなければならないこと→仕事」

(b) puzzle は「〜を困惑させる」だから *be* puzzled で「困惑する」。not 〜 in the least「少しも〜ない」

全文訳　インド人は時間のことを気にしないように思える。インド人の生活様式を見ていると，「時は金なり」ということわざの意味を理解できるかどうか知りたくなってくる。彼らの生活は時間など気にもかけずに，ゆっくり進ん

でいるように思える。

　　私はかつてボンベイ(現ムンバイ)へ行く切符を買うため，ニューデリーの航空会社の切符売場に出かけた。人々は長い列をいくつも作って順番を待っていたけれども，長い間待たされているのをまるで気にしていないようだった。一方(a)若い女性の係員は，人々の列も気にせずに，美しいサリーをしとやかになびかせながら，のんびりと職務についていた。私はたった 1 枚の切符を予約するのにほぼ 3 時間かかった。すぐそのあとで，電報電話会社での電報業務でも同じことであるとわかった。私はボンベイのインド人の友人に空港に私を迎えに来てほしかったから，彼宛てに電報を打ってもらった。しかし係員がのろのろと仕事を進めているのを見て，その日のうちに友人のところへ電報が届かないかもしれないと心配になりだした。

　　私の心配は現実になったのだ！　その次の夜，私がボンベイ空港に着いたとき，友人は見当たらなかった。ついに何とか私はその友人の家へ行く道を見つけたが，結局のところ，電報はまだ配達されていないということを聞いた。(b)私の友人が少しも驚いているように見えないのに私は戸惑った。電報はその次の日の午後，配達された。すなわち，私が電報を打ってから丸 2 日後のことだった。

　　いつも急いで仕事をしている日本人の立場からは，インド人の生活は不便なように思えるが，それがまったく不便だと彼らが感じていないことに着目することは，とても興味深い。私たち日本人は種々の約束や仕事にいつも追い立てられて，行動を時間の枠の中へ無理に押し込める。一方インド人の生活は，時間のゆったりとした経過とともに，のんびりと進んでいるように思える。この同じ地球上で何と大きな違いだろう！

Point

〈have ＋目的語＋過去分詞 / 原形不定詞〉（使役）

① I had *my desk* mended by my father.

② I had *my father* mend my desk.

（私は父に机を修理してもらった。）

解説

　　どちらの文も意味は同じである。目的語が「物」のときは**過去分詞**が続き，「人」のときは**原形不定詞**が続く。

　　①の文では「机」と「修理する」が受動関係にあるから過去分詞 mended に，②の文では「父」と「修理する」が能動関係にあるから原形不定詞 mend になると考えればよい。

05 人間の役に立つ昆虫　(pp. 12〜13)

(1)　(A)**ウ**　(B)**イ**　(C)**ア**　(D)**エ**　(E)**オ**
(2)　(a)**ウ**　(b)**ア**　(c)**ア**　(d)**ウ**
(3)　①雑草を除去する目的で昆虫が利用でき
　　　るという側面。(24 字)
　　　②増えすぎたサボテンを食べ，ほかの植
　　　物には害を及ぼさない昆虫。(30 字)
(4)　the rabbit multiplied prodigiously and
　　developed into a very serious problem

解説

(1)(A)「両方の場合に」in 〜 case は「〜の場合に」。
(B)「これらの理由により」for 〜 reason は「〜の理
由により」。　(C)「1 年に 100 万エーカーの速さで」
「速さ・割合」を表す at を用いる。　(D)「依存」を表
す on が入る。　(E)「ウチワサボテンが足りなくなっ
たせいで」owing to 〜 で「〜のせいで」。
(2)(a)「悪名高い」　(b)「大量に」　(c)「食べることができ
る」　(d)「〜を再生，再利用する」
(3)①「物事の違う側面」直後の文に書かれている，昆
虫が有益であるという側面を指す。　②「『安全な』昆
虫の種」直前の文の内容から判断する。人間にとっ
て有益な植物を食べる昆虫は『安全』ではない。
(4)「ウサギをオーストラリアへ連れてきたことはなぜ
間違いだったか。」第 2 段落第 3 文(*ll.* 9-10)に「天敵
がいなく，繁殖しすぎて大問題になった」とある。

全文訳
　　一般的に人間は昆虫を味方というよりも敵とみ
なし，科学者は昆虫によって引き起こされる一見無限と思
える数々の問題を解決するのにかなりの時間を費やしてい
る。しかし，物事には違った側面がある。昆虫は厄介な雑
草の繁殖を食い止めたり，抑制したりするのに使われる場
合がある。
　　人間は外来種の植物や野生動物を国内に入れると，その
地域の自然の均衡が破壊される危険性をたいへんひどい目
にあって学んできた。オーストラリア国内にウサギを持ち
込んだことは，この不名誉な例のひとつである。それほど
知られていないがほとんど同じように深刻な問題となった
のが，オーストラリアにウチワサボテンを持ち込んだこと
である。ウサギもサボテンも繁殖を抑制するような明らか
な天敵がいなかった。その結果，大量繁殖し，たいへん深
刻な問題となった。どちらの場合も結果的に繁殖を抑制で
きたのは主として昆虫を国内に持ち込んだおかげであっ
た——蚊が致死性の病をウサギに広め，蛾がサボテンを食
い尽くしたのである。
　　ウチワサボテンの多くの種は中南米の原産である。それ
らは垣根に使う植物として便利で，その実は食べられる。
これらの理由により世界の多くの地域に持ち込まれたのだ
が，結果がよくないこともたびたびあった。オーストラリ
アでは気候と土壌が適していたため，サボテンはすぐに繁
殖し始めた。1919 年に最も広まったときにはおよそ 6,000

万エーカーもの肥沃な土地が不毛の土地となり，1 年に
100 万エーカーの速さでサボテンは広がっていると見積も
られた。
　　1920 年にはウチワサボテンと関連のある昆虫を調査す
るために科学者が派遣された。全部で 145 種類の昆虫が
発見され，それらのすべてがウチワサボテンや別の種のサ
ボテンをえさとしていた。
　　それらの昆虫の中からかなり多くの昆虫がトマト，モモ，
リンゴ，イチジク，バナナも食べて生きることがわかった
ので，それらは却下されなければならなかった。最終的に
約 18 種類の「安全な」種が検証のために選定された。それ
らのいく種かが何とかオーストラリアに住みついて，1 つ
の種，アルゼンチン原産の蛾がウチワサボテンの最も強い
天敵となった。
　　1935 年までにほとんどすべてのサボテンが根こそぎ駆
除された。そのとき以来，蛾の数は，ウチワサボテンが足
りなくなったせいで元の数のうち，ほんの少しの数に減っ
た。しかし，蛾は条件がよければすぐに増える力があるため，
ウチワサボテンを自然に抑制する役割を続けている。失わ
れた何万エーカーもの土地は再生され，今では放牧や農耕
にフル活用されている。

Point

現在完了
① 完了
　Human beings have learned the danger of
　upsetting the natural balance.
　（人間は自然の均衡が崩れることの危険性を学
　んできた。）
② 経験
　I have never been to Okinawa.
　（私は沖縄に行ったことがない。）
③ 継続
　We have known each other for about ten
　years.
　（私たちはほぼ 10 年来の知り合いです。）
④ 結果
　My father has gone to Tokyo on business.
　（私の父は仕事で東京へ行ってしまった。）

解説
　**現在完了〈have [has] ＋過去分詞〉には完了・
経験・継続・結果の 4 用法がある。**
④の「結果」は過去に起きた動作・出来事の現在
における状況[結果]を表し，「〜した結果，今は
…である」という意味が含まれる。上の例文では
「東京に行ってしまって，今はここにいない」とい
う意味を含んでいる。これに対し，単に過去形
で My father went to Tokyo on business. と表さ
れる場合は，「東京へ行った」という事実を述べて
いるだけであり，今どこにいるのかという内容は
まったく含まれないことに注意すること。
　現在完了の受身は〈have [has] ＋ been ＋過去

〈分詞〉である。

- The prickly-pear cacti **have been introduced** into many parts of the world.
（ウチワサボテンは世界の多くの地域に持ち込まれた。）〈完了〉

06 正直さを生み出す2つの要因 (pp. 14〜15)

(1) ①**イ** ②**エ** ③**ウ**
(2) **エ**
(3) **ウ，カ**

解説

(1)①「一生のうちで盗みもズルもしないことが肝心だ」 **ア**「重要でない」，**ウ**「生まれつきの」，**エ**「洗練された」 ②直前の know の目的語にあたる間接疑問。疑問詞のあとは〈主語＋動詞〉の語順となる。 ③「第2の要因は愛着だ」 **ア**「判断（力），分別」，**イ**「特権，特典」，**エ**「得意分野，特徴」
(2)下線部は最終段落第1文(*ll.* 23-24)の people are more honest when they care about the seller in some way を指す。**エ**「客が売り手に対して好感を抱いていると，その売り手との取引でより正直になる」
(3)**ウ**「農家の門前にある良心箱に似た仕組みは，公共交通機関の料金の支払いで試しに使われたことは一度もない」 第2段落第3文(*ll.* 9-10)に不一致。
カ「2枚の異なるポスターを使った実験では，愛着が人々の正直さを決める2つの主な要因のひとつであることが証明された」 第4段落の内容に不一致。

全文訳
私たちはみな，正直がいちばんだと教わる。本当のことを話すのは大事なことで，一生のうちで盗みもズルもしないことが肝心だ。あなたが私にどれくらい正直かたずねたとしたら，私は「いつだって本当に正直です」と答えるだろう。たしかに私はそのような自分でありたいし……おそらくほとんどの人がそうでありたいだろう。しかし，良心箱の仕組みに注目すると，状況によっては，人は自分が思いたいほど正直ではない。では，何が人の正直さを決めるのか。

良心箱はよく駅で新聞や，農家の門前で野菜のような品物を売るのに使われる。あなたはほしいものを手に取り，お金を箱に入れて支払う。ときには，同じようなやりかたがバスや電車で運賃を支払うのに使われる。このような仕組みは，長い列ができるのを防ぐので，よくできたものだ。しかし，売る側にとってはリスクになる。だれかがお金を払わなかったとしても，売る側はその客がだれなのかわからないだろう。

良心箱は今や，オンラインの世界にも組み込まれている。2007年，レディオヘッドはニューアルバム *In Rainbows* をデジタル版の良心箱を使って販売することにした。彼らがダウンロード版としてアルバムをリリースすると，空白

になった料金欄が画面に現れて，こう表示された。「きみにまかせる」ほとんどの人が適正な金額を支払った。

この場合，ほとんどの人が正直だったのはなぜか。人の正直さを決める主な要因は2つある。まず，だれかが見ていると思えば，人はより正直になる。この説を検証するために，研究者たちが実験を行った。1枚のポスターが，とあるオフィスの紅茶とコーヒー用の良心箱の上に貼られ，異なる2枚のポスターが検証された。1枚は花，もう1枚は2つの眼が映ったものだ。検証結果からわかったのは，ポスターが2つの眼だったとき，人はポスターが花であるときより正直だったことだ。彼らは言うまでもなく，だれかが自分を見ていると感じたのだ。

第2の要因は愛着だ。何らかの形で売る側のことを大事に思うとき，人はより正直になる。レディオヘッドのアルバムを購入した人は誠実な客であり，レディオヘッドの心からのファンだったのだろう。この考えを検証するために，別の実験で，買い物客がつり銭を多く手渡された。たいていの人はおつりを確かめて，多く渡されたり少なく渡されたりすると，すぐ気づく。検証の結果からわかったのは，大型スーパーマーケットでは，ほとんどの場合，余分なおつりを懐にしまい込んだことだ。一方，小さな店では，人はより正直になり，余分なおつりを返した。さて，あなたはどうか。自分がそうありたいと思うほど，あなたは正直だろうか。

Point

間接疑問文
① Scientists hope to study **when the asteroid was formed**.
（科学者たちは，その小惑星がいつ形成されたのか研究したいと望んでいる。）
② Scientists hope to study **how solar wind and radiation have affected it**.
（科学者たちは，太陽風と放射線がそれにどのような影響を与えてきたのか，研究したいと望んでいる。）

解説
間接疑問文では，通常の疑問文とは語順が変わる点に注意。（主語の前に be，have，do そのほかの助動詞がこない）
① When *was* **the asteroid** formed?
→ Scientists hope to study when **the asteroid *was*** formed.
② How *have* **solar wind and radiation** affected it?
→ Scientists hope to study how **solar wind and radiation *have*** affected it.
①の場合，元の疑問文では主語の the asteroid の前に be(was)がくる。②の場合，元の疑問文では主語の solar wind and radiation の前に have がくる。
・ただし，疑問詞が主語の場合は，同じ語順になる。

Who *will* win the first prize?
→ I do not know **who** *will* win the first prize.
（だれが１等を取るか，私にはわかりません。）

07 オープンラーニング　　(pp. 16〜17)

(1)　**ウ**　　(2)　**ウ**
(3)　**ア**
(4)　**全文訳** の下線部参照。
(5)　**イ**　　(6)　**ア**

解説

(1) Some adults 〜 school まで が 主部。may wish to do so の so は「大学へ行って勉強すること(go to college or university)」を指す。but find they cannot のあとに do so (= go to college or university) が省略されている。
(2) correspondence courses は「通信教育(課程)」のこと。**ウ**は第２段落最終文 (*ll.* 15-16) に不一致。
(3) 空所の直後に「授業を始める前に準備コースを受ける」とあることから，**ア**「大学に入学するための標準資格を持っていない場合は」が入る。
(4) principle の直後の that は接続詞で，同格を表す。the principle と further 〜 everyone が同格関係にあり，「さらなる教育があらゆる人に開かれているべきだという原則」という意味。
(5) 第３段落ではイギリスのオープンユニバーシティについて，第４段落ではアメリカでのそれに代わる教育について述べられている。
(6) **ア**「生涯教育」　**イ**「古典教育」　**ウ**「義務教育」
　　エ「初等教育」

全文訳　　大学に進まずに学業を終える成人の中には，人生においてあとで通いたいと思っても仕事や家事に追われたり，お金が不足していたりするために大学に通えないことに気づく人もいるだろう。オープンラーニング計画によって，自分の都合のいい時間に家庭で勉強して，どんな水準の教育コースでも受けることができるようになっている。オープンラーニングでは，ほとんどの学生は授業を受けるために教育施設に行かずに自宅で学習するため，ときには遠隔教育とも呼ばれている。
　ざっくばらんに言えば，オープンラーニングにはテレビ番組を見て語学を学ぶことや講座関連の本で勉強することも含まれるだろう。専門職の資格や学位を取るためのオープンラーニングはしばしば通信教育に基づいて行われている。そのような教育課程は「オープンラーニング」という用語が 1970 年代によく知られるようになる前から存在していたのだが。通信教育の受講生は印刷された教材を郵送で受け取り，指導教員に課題を送って添削してもらう。通信教育にはそのほかに，一度にすべての学習教材を受け取り，学生がそれをすべて自分自身で学習するといったものもあ

る。今ではインターネットを通じて学習できる課程や連続したテレビ番組を定期視聴して学習する課程もある。受講には費用がかかるが，仕事をやめて全日制で学ぶ場合よりも総費用はずっと少ない。
　イギリスで最もよく知られているオープンラーニング施設はオープンユニバーシティであり，1969 年に設立された。そこではイギリスとヨーロッパ連合の国々からの学生を受け入れている。学生に年齢制限はなく，大学に入学するための標準資格を持っていない場合は，授業を始める前に準備コースを受ける。授業は印刷された教材とテレビやラジオ番組の受講を合わせた形で行われる。学生は自宅で学習し，課題を指導教員に郵送する。多くの学生は自分の町の教育センターに月ごとの個人授業を受けに行く。またサマースクールにも出席できる。受講するのに期限はないが，ほとんどの学生は４，５年に及ぶ定時制の学位課程を取る。大学院課程や専門職課程も受講できる。1990 年代半ばまでにオープンユニバーシティの受講生は約 20 万人にのぼり，ここでの成功によって世界のほかの地域でも同様の教育機関が開設されるに至っている。
　アメリカ合衆国ではオープンユニバーシティのような国の機関はないが，<u>さらなる教育があらゆる人に開かれているべきだという原則が広く受け入れられていて，多くの教育の機会がある</u>。多くの大学が通信教育を行っており，たいていの大学，とくに州政府によって運営されている大学には，いろいろな手段が用意されていて，それにより，関心のある人は大学で学ぶことができる。

Point

同　格
① **同格の that**
No one can deny the fact **that** you are guilty.
（あなたが有罪であるという事実をだれも否定できない。）
The rumor **that** the teacher was absent turned out to be false.
（先生が休みだといううわさは間違いだとわかった。）
② **同格の of**
Everyone agreed to the idea **of** having a farewell party.
（みんながお別れパーティーをするという考えに同意した。）
③ **同格の to 不定詞**
She has a strong desire **to be** a designer.
（彼女はデザイナーになるという強い希望を持っている。）
解説
　①〈名詞＋ that 節〉の形で「〜という 名詞 」のように名詞の内容を that 節が説明する。このときの名詞には thought，fact，idea，rumor，belief，plan，opinion などがある。
　②〈名詞 A ＋ of ＋名詞 B〔動名詞(句)〕〉の形で

「B という A」を表す。

③〈名詞＋ to 不定詞〉の形で「～という **名詞** 」のように名詞の内容を不定詞が説明する。このときに使われる名詞は plan，wish，desire などである。

08 動物の自己認識　　　(pp. 18～19)

(1) **エ**　　(2) **エ**
(3) (c)**ア**　(f)**イ**
(4) (d)**イ**　(e)**ア**
(5) ①**ウ**　②**ア**

解説

(1) 2 つあとの文に Are animals self-aware? とある。
(2)「たとえマークテストに<u>彼らが</u>合格していなくても」チンパンジーやオランウータンは合格しているので，「ほかの種」を指す。
(3) (c) make sense「理にかなう」　(f) at issue「論争中で」
この文は倒置になっている。the degree ～ creatures が主語。is が動詞。
(4) (d) all the animal has to work with is a flipper「その動物が使うために持っているのはヒレだけである」all は「すべてのもの」の意味の代名詞で，all のあとに関係代名詞 that が省略されていて，the animal has to work with が all を修飾している。
(e) free of ～「～を免れて」　否定語 hardly がつくと「ほとんど避けられない」。
(5)①**ウ**「3 歳児の大多数は自分の頭にステッカーがついていることに気づかない」　②**ア**「ある動物がマークテストに合格しない理由の 1 つとして，<u>身体機能の不足</u>が考えられる」

全文訳

哲学者のトマス・ネーゲルは「コウモリであるとはどのようなことか」という質問を以前に投げかけた。想像してみよう。暗やみだ。たくさんのキーキー鳴く声が聞こえる。飛んでいる。ほんの少し……コウモリらしく感じてきた。でも，待てよ。コウモリには自分がコウモリだという意識はあるのか。この点に関して，犬，牛，類人猿の心には何が起こっているのか。動物は自己を認識しているのだろうか。

1960 年代のある日，心理学者ゴードン・ギャラップは鏡の前でひげをそっているときに，動物を鏡の前に立たせたらどうするだろうかと考えた。彼はマークテストと呼ぶものを考案し，そのテストにおいて，鏡と鏡に映る自分の姿に慣れている類人猿が麻酔で眠らされ，片方の眉と片方の耳の上のところに染料でマークをつけられた。麻酔からさめると，動物たちは鏡に映る自分の姿を見せられた。

チンパンジーとオランウータンの 2 つの種は毛染めした場所を触って反応した——これらの種が自己を認識している証拠だとギャラップは論じた。しかし，ハーバード大学

の生物学者ドナルド・グリフィンは，ほかの種も自己を認識していると考えている。たとえマークテストに彼らが合格していなくても。チンパンジーとオランウータンがテストに合格して，一方でゴリラのようなほかの類人猿が合格しないのは理屈に合わないとグリフィンは言う。それに，大人のチンパンジーの 75 パーセントだけがテストに合格する。「自己を認識しているチンパンジーもいれば，認識していないものもいると言うべきです。ちょっとばかげた感じでしょ」とグリフィンは言う。

イルカもギャラップのマークテストの形を変えたテストに合格できると考えている研究者もいるが，その動物に動かせるものがヒレだけであるとき，テストは難しくなる。この研究領域においては，何についてであれ論争は避けがたい。

人間がほかの動物とどの程度異なっているかが論争中だ。我々は特別なのか，それともただ自己中心的なのか。

ルイジアナ大学の科学者ダニエル・ポビネッリは，マークテストに合格する幼児でさえ，年長の子どもが持っているような自己認識に欠けると論じている。ポビネッリの実験のひとつで，幼児たちは，数分前に何者かがこっそり彼らの頭に大きくて色鮮やかなステッカーを貼りつける映像を見る。ほとんどの 3 歳児は，映像を見てすぐに手を伸ばし，ステッカーをはがすことができない。自分が映っているのはわかっても，自分の頭にステッカーがまだ貼りついていることをしっかり理解できるわけではないのだ。しかし，ほとんどの 4 歳児はこのテストに合格する。

このマークテストで本当に何が測れているのか確かなことは言えない。意識と自己認識に関する研究はわからないことだらけである。例えば，ある動物は，単にマークに触れるためのまともな筋力がないという理由でテストに合格しないことも考えられるのではないか。科学では，興味深い答えを得ることもあるが，私たちの問うたものがいったい何であったのか，きちんと判断できないこともある。

Point

〈前置詞＋関係代名詞 **目的格** 〉
① That is the house **in which** they lived.
（あれは彼らが住んでいた家である。）
② Charlotte never failed to get something **on which** she set her heart.
（シャーロットは自分のものにしたいと思ったものを必ず手に入れた。）

解説

〈前置詞＋関係代名詞〉の表現は，次のように書き換えができる。
①＝③ That is the house **which** they lived **in**.
（＝ That is the house. They lived in the house.）
②＝④ Charlotte never failed to get something **which** she set her heart **on**.
（＝Charlotte never failed to get something. She set her heart on something.）
前置詞が関係代名詞節の最後に置かれた場合

（③と④）は，関係代名詞 which は，省略することができる。また，この場合は関係代名詞 that に書き換えることもできる。しかし，〈前置詞＋関係代名詞〉の形のとき（①と②）は，省略することも that に置き換えることもできない。

09 女性解放運動　　　　　(pp. 20〜21)

(1)　①イ　②ウ　③エ
(2)　全文訳 の下線部①，②参照。

全文訳 の下線部①，②参照。

解説

(1)①その当時，女性はお金を稼ぐことは許されていたが，所有することは許されていなかった。　②スーザンと彼女の支持者は女性解放運動に乗り出した。　③スーザンは大統領選挙で女性も投票すべきだと主張した。
(2)① take it for granted that 〜 は「〜を当然のことと思う」の意味。it は形式目的語。　②やや日本語にしにくいので，工夫が必要。ring out「響き渡る」with は様態を表す。

全文訳　①今日，私たちは女性に男性と同様の選挙権があることを当然のことと思っている。女性は自分が稼ぐお金を所有することができる。結婚していようと独身だろうと，財産を所有することができる。女性が大学へ行き，自分の選ぶどんな業種や職業にも就けるのは当然のことと考えられている。しかし，今日の女性が享受しているこれらの権利は，女性の自由を求めた多くの闘士たちの勇敢な努力によって，そして何よりも偉大なスーザン・B・アンソニーによって，獲得された。

　100 年ほど前，アメリカの女性はお金を稼ぐことはできたが，それを所有することは許されていなかった。もし女性が結婚していて，仕事に就けば，稼いだお金はすべて彼女の夫の財産になった。夫はその家族の完全な主人と考えられていた。彼の妻は明瞭に考えることもできない愚か者とみなされ，それゆえに法律は，彼女が幸運にも所有できた財産に後見人――もちろん男性の後見人――を立てることで彼女を寛大に保護したのだった。

　スーザン・アンソニーのような女性たちはこの不公平に激怒した。スーザンは女性がそのように扱われるべき理由がわからなかった。

　1872 年の大統領選挙の日，スーザンを含む 15 人の女性が建物の前に集まった。「私は合衆国大統領の投票をするためにここにやって来ました。彼はあなた方の大統領になるだけでなく，私の大統領にもなります。私たちはこの国を守る子どもたちを産む女性です。私たちはあなた方の家庭を築き，あなた方の食事を作り，あなた方の息子や娘を育てる女性です。私たち女性はあなた方とまったく同様に，この国の国民ですから，私たちは自分たちの指導者となる人に投票することを要求します」と彼女は言った。

彼女の言葉は②鐘の音のようにはっきりと響いた。そしてその言葉は心を打った。それから，押し黙り堂々とした態度で，スーザンは投票箱につかつかと歩み寄り，自分の票を記した用紙を投票箱に入れた。ほかの 14 人の女性もそれぞれ同じ行動をとった。

　1872 年のその重要な日に，スーザン・B・アンソニーと彼女の忠実な支持者は，合衆国大統領に対する最初の投票を象徴的な形で行った。彼女はアメリカ人女性の権利の最も偉大な擁護者であった。

Point

関係代名詞 what
① She always does **what** is right.
（彼女は常に正しいことをする。）
② This is **what** happened in the past.
（これが過去に起こったことだ。）
③ He is not **what he was**.
（彼は昔の彼ではない。）
④ He is **what is called** a walking dictionary.
（彼はいわゆる生き字引だ。）
⑤ Reading is to the mind **what** food is to the body.
（読書の精神に対する関係は食物の体に対する関係と同じである。）

解説
　what は 1 語で〈先行詞＋関係代名詞〉の働きをし，「〜すること[もの]」の意味を表す。what ＝ the thing(s) which, the thing(s) that と考えるとよい。what 〜 は名詞節なので，①のように目的語，②のように補語となり，主語にもなる。
・**What** I said wasn't true.
（私が言ったことは真実ではなかった。）
　関係代名詞 what を使った慣用表現も覚えておこう。
③〈**what**（＋人）＋ **is**〉は「現在の（人）」，〈**what**（＋人）＋ **was**[**used to be**]〉は「過去の（人）」。
④ **what is called 〜** は「いわゆる」。
⑤ **A is to B what C is to D** は「A の B に対する関係は C の D に対する関係と同じである」。

10 大都市の交通渋滞　　(pp. 22〜23)

- (1) (A)**イ** (B)**ウ** (C)**エ** (D)**ア** (E)**オ**
- (2) ①**イ** ②**ウ** ③**イ**
- (3) **エ**
- (4) 全文訳 の下線部参照。
- (5) **イ，ウ**

解説

(1)(A) deal with 〜「〜に対処する」 (B) in the first place 「まず，第 1 に」 (C) famous for 〜「〜で有名な」 (E) on the way「途中で」

(2)① the number of 〜「〜の数」 a number of 〜「たくさんの〜」 even number「偶数」 odd number「奇数」
② in addition「さらに，それに加えて」 on the contrary「逆に」 シンガポール政府が行ったこと 3 つのうちの 2 番目なので，finally「最後に」，thirdly 「3 番目に」は不可。 ③動詞を強調する do。現在行われていることについての言及なので，過去形，未来形は不可。主語が many (countries)で複数なので，does も不可。

(3) fine「〜に罰金を科す」

(4) according to whether 〜「〜かどうかによって」 license plate「(自動車の)ナンバープレート」 〈seem to have ＋過去分詞〉は時制に注意する。

(5)**ア**「言及されている都市の中で，バンコクだけは，ひどい交通渋滞に悩まされていない」バンコクも，ひどい渋滞の起きている都市の例として挙げられている。 **イ**「ジャカルタであなたは，車に乗るだけでお金を稼げるかもしれない」第 4 段落参照。頭数(あたまかず)を揃えるために「3 人目の人」になるというアルバイトが登場した。 **ウ**「アテネでは，大気汚染がある古代の神殿にダメージを与えている」第 5 段落参照。 **エ**「オーストラリアでは，『トランジット・レーン』のシステムが，すべての人に支持されている」不満を言っている人もいる。

全文訳
日本人はしばしば，「日本でひどい交通渋滞が起こるのは，日本は小さいのに，あまりにも多くの車があるためだ」と主張する。しかし，世界の大都市ではどこでも，状況は同じである。バンコク，北京，メキシコシティー，アテネのような場所は，交通渋滞と排気ガスで有名であり，この問題に終わりはないようだ。

シンガポールでは，都市の中心部に入るすべての車に通行税を課すことにより，この状況に賢く対処してきた。日中，このエリアに入りたいドライバーは，料金所でお金を払ってフロントガラスに貼りつけるカードを受け取る。万一，料金を払わずに中に入ってしまった場合，料金所のオペレーターの 1 人が車のナンバーを記録して，後日，あなたは罰金を科されることになる。

まず，シンガポール政府が国内の車の数に制限を加えてしまったため，車を買いたい人は，所有許可証を得られる

まで待たなければならない。さらに，車を所有するためのコストには，許可取得にかかるお金，税金，車両そのものの値段が含まれ，1,000 万円に届く可能性がある。そのうえ，ガソリンの値段がとても高く，隣国マレーシアのおよそ 2 倍もする。このような事情があるにもかかわらず，多くのシンガポール人は，それでも車を所有したいようである。

ほかの国々では状況はそれほど厳しくはないとしても，多くの国に何らかの形で交通規制の仕組みがある。インドネシアのジャカルタでは，昼間に主要道路を走る場合，運転者を含めて少なくとも 3 人が乗車している必要がある。この頭数を満たすため，「3 人目の人」になるというアルバイトが出現した。

ギリシャの首都アテネは，古代のパルテノン神殿で有名であるが，町の中心部の近くに位置しているため，この神殿は排気ガスによってダメージを受けている。この市では，ナンバープレートの最後の数字が奇数か偶数かによって車の使用を規制するシステムがあるが，ほとんど効果はなかったようである。

オーストラリアは，車なしでは不便な国である。車の数を減らすため政府は「トランジット・レーン」を導入し，3 人以上が乗っている車に優先権を与えた。しかし，この制度が制定されてから，途中で近所の人を乗せる一方で，わざわざその人の家に行くとなると，片道 30 分余計にかかることがあると，不満を言う人もいる。

日本では，今のところこのような交通システムは存在していないが，ほかの国々でこれらのシステムが引き起こしている不都合を考えると，このような規制を導入すべきか否かを決めるのは難しい問題である。

Point

seem to 不定詞
① She **seems to be** asleep.
（彼女は眠っているようだ。）
② She **seems to have been** asleep.
（彼女は眠っていたようだ。）

解説
〈seem ＋ to 不定詞〉の表現を非人称の it で始まる文で書き換えると，次のようになる。
①＝ It **seems** that she is asleep.
（＝ She **seems** to be asleep.）
不定詞で表していた部分がisになることに注意。
②＝ It **seems** that she was asleep.
（＝ She **seems** to have been asleep.）
seem の後に完了不定詞を使うと seem と時制のずれがあることを示し，不定詞で表していた部分が was になることに注意。

11 人間の脳 (pp. 24〜25)

(1) (A)**イ** (B)**エ** (C)**ウ**
(2) ①**エ** ②**ア** ③**ウ**
(3) remarkable
(4) **ウ，エ**

解説

(1)(A) believe it or not「信じようが信じまいが，信じられないかもしれないが」 (B)「しかしあなたはそれを，すぐにマスターしてしまう」と続くので，「自転車に乗ることは，最初は不可能に見える」の意味になる impossible を選ぶ。fun「楽しい」 exhausting「疲れる」 (C) over and over「何度も何度も」 over and above 〜「〜に加えて」 over and done「すっかり終わって」 over and out「交信終わり」

(2) ① complicated「複雑な」 simplistic「単純な」 theatrical「劇場の，芝居じみた」 inferior「劣った」 ② whole world「全世界」 tiresome「疲れる」 encircled「取り囲まれた」 entry-level「入門レベルの」 ③ bare foot「素足」 naked「裸の」 candid「率直な，包み隠さない」 bear-like「クマのような」 athlete's foot「水虫」

(3) remarkable「すばらしい，注目に値する」

(4)**ア**「運動をしたあと，あなたの脳はあまりよく機能しない」最終段落参照。むしろ，理解力が上がる。
　イ「あなたが眠っているとき，脳の活動は短時間停止する」第3段落参照。脳の活動は停止しない。
　ウ「運動神経は感覚神経より速く情報を伝達することができる」 運動神経は時速200マイル以上，感覚神経は時速150マイル以上。第4段落参照。
　エ「感情を持つには，脳は必要不可欠である」第1段落参照。

全文訳

あなたは，3ポンド（1.4キログラム）の，あなたがするであろうことすべてを制御している，しわの多い物質のかたまりを頭の中に収めて持ち歩いている。あなたが考え，学習し，創造し，感情を持つことを可能にすることから，すべてのまばたき，呼吸，心臓の鼓動を制御することに至るまで——このすばらしいコントロールセンターが，あなたの脳である。それは，あまりにも驚異的な構造物であるので，ある有名な科学者はかつてそれを「我々が今までにこの世界で発見した中で，最も複雑なもの」と呼んだ。

あなたの飼い猫がキッチンのカウンターの上にいる。彼女は，熱いコンロを今にも踏みそうだ。あなたが行動できる時間はほんの数秒だ。あなたの脳は，目から入ってきた信号にアクセスし，彼女を捕まえるには，いつ，どこへ，どのくらいの速度で飛び込む必要があるか，すばやく計算する。そして，あなたの脳は筋肉に，そうするように命令を出す。あなたのタイミングは完璧で，彼女は危機を脱する。目，耳，そのほかの感覚器官から入ってくる大量の

情報をダウンロードし，処理し，反応する，あなたの脳の驚くべき能力には，どんなコンピュータもかなわない。

あなたの脳には約1,000億個の神経細胞がある。あまりにもたくさんあるので，すべてを数えようとしたら3,000年以上かかるであろう。いつあなたが夢を見たり，笑ったり，考えたり，見たり，動いたりしようとも，それは，わずかな化学物質や電気信号が，何十億という小さな神経細胞のハイウェイに沿って，神経細胞の間を高速で走り回っているからである。信じられないかもしれないが，あなたの脳内の活動は，決して止まることはない。毎秒，数え切れないほどのメッセージがその中で，勢いづいたピンボールゲーム機のように行き交っている。あなたの神経細胞は，世界中のすべての電話でやり取りされているよりも多くのメッセージを作り，送り出している。そして，1つの神経細胞が作り出す電気の量はごくわずかであるが，あなたの神経細胞すべてを合わせれば，低ワット数の電球を光らせるのに十分な電気を作り出せる。

1匹のハチがあなたの素足にとまる。あなたの皮膚にある感覚神経はこの情報を脊髄と脳へ時速150マイル（240キロ）以上の速さで伝達する。するとあなたの脳は運動神経を使い，そのハチをすばやく振り払うように，脊髄を通してあなたの足へメッセージを送り返す。運動神経はこの情報を，時速200マイル（320キロ）以上の速さで伝達することができる。

自転車に乗ることは，最初は不可能に見える。しかし，あなたはすぐにそれをマスターしてしまう。どうやって？練習をするとき，あなたの脳は「自転車に乗る」メッセージを，ある神経細胞の通り道に沿って繰り返し繰り返し送り，その結果，新しい神経接続が形成される。実際，あなたの脳の構造は，あなたが学習するたびに，新しい考えや記憶を持つたびに変化する。

ランニングやバスケットボールのような，心拍数を上げる運動はどんなものでも，体にとてもよく，また，あなたの気分をよくする助けにさえなることはよく知られている。しかし，科学者たちは最近，運動後しばらくの間，あなたの脳の学習能力をより高める化学物質が体内で作られることを発見した。だから，もしあなたが宿題の問題で行き詰まったなら，外に出てサッカーの試合をし，そのあと改めて問題に挑んでみるといい。あなたは，自分がその問題を解けることに気づくかもしれない。

Point

分詞構文
① **Walking** along the street, I met a friend of mine.
　（通りを歩いていると，私の友達に会った。）
② **Born** in France, he is proficient in French.
　（フランスで生まれたので，彼はフランス語が上手だ。）

解説

分詞構文は文脈とともに意味が理解される表現で，やや文語的なものである。ふつう従属接続詞

のいずれかに置き換えて読むとうまく読める。それぞれ，次のように置き換えることができる。
① = When I was walking along the street, 〜.
② = As he was born in France, 〜.
　ただし，次のような付帯状況（〜しながら）の分詞構文がその基本形である。
・**Walking** on tiptoe, I approached the door.
（つまさきで歩きながら，私は扉に近づいた。）
・"I must go now," he said, **smiling** at me.
（「もう行かなければならない」と彼は私の方にほほえみかけながら言った。）

12 国際語が生まれる条件　(pp. 26〜27)

(1)　①**イ**　③**ア**　④**エ**
(2)　最初：Why　最後：language
(3)　国際語とは，文学的要素や表現の明瞭さの点において理想的な模範である。(34字)
(4)　English　　(5)　**エ**
(6)　**ア，イ，オ**

解説

(1)① has little to do with 〜は「〜とはほとんど関係がない」。be connected with 〜「〜と結びつけられる」
③ thanks to 〜 は「〜のおかげで」。owing to 〜 も同じ意味。　④ apart from 〜 は「〜から離れて」independent of 〜「〜から独立して，離れて」
(2)直前の文の主語「なぜある言語が国際語になるのか」を指す。
(3)下線部⑤の popular and misleading beliefs は「よく知られていて，誤解を招く恐れのある考え」という意味。この内容は直後の文の that 以下 an international 〜 expression に書かれている。
(4)この段落後半は「英語」についての話題。
(5)下線部⑦は「言語は，その言語に備っている構造的な特性によって国際語になるのではない」という意味。
(6)**ア**「その言語を使う国の政府の権力」第1段落第4文（*ll.* 4-5）と一致。　**イ**「その言語を使う人々の高い水準の技術力」第2段落第1文（*ll.* 8-9）に一致する。**オ**「その言語が使われる国の軍事力」最終段落最終文（*ll.* 31-32）の内容に一致する。

全文訳　ある言語が国際語になる理由は，それを話す人の数とはほとんど関係がない。それを話す人がだれなのかということのほうが大きく関係する。ラテン語はローマ帝国全体で国際語となったが，これはローマ人の数が，彼らが征服した人々の数よりも多かったからではなかった。単により強力な力があったからだ。のちに，ローマ帝国の軍事力が衰退したとき，ラテン語は 1,000 年間，教育にお

いての国際語として残った。それは別の種類の力，すなわち，ローマ・カトリック教の宗教的な影響力のおかげだ。
　言語の優位性と経済力，技術力，文化的な支配力の間にも密接なつながりがある。どういった種類であれ，強力な基盤がないと，どんな言語も国際的な意思伝達手段の媒体として発展することはできない。言語は，それを話す人から切り離され，謎めいたような空間にとどまりながら独立して存在しているのではない。言語はそれを使う人の脳，口，耳，手，目の中にのみ存在する。言語を使う人が国際舞台で成功すれば，その言語も成功する。彼らが失敗すれば，その言語も失敗する。
　この点は自明なことに思えるかもしれないが，明確にしておく必要がある。なぜなら，ある言語が国際的に成功する理由について，よく耳にする誤解を招く恐れのある多くの考えが，長年にわたって広まってきたからだ。国際語とは，文学的要素や表現の明瞭さの点において理想的な模範であると人々が主張するのをよく耳にする。ヘブライ語，ギリシャ語，ラテン語，アラビア語，フランス語は，さまざまな時代にそのような言葉で賞賛されてきた言語の中に入り，英語も例外ではない。例えば，英語が今日とても広く使われている理由を説明するために，英語の構造自体に本質的に美しい何か，もしくは論理的な何かがあるに違いないということがしばしば指摘される。「英語はほかの言語よりも文法が少ない」と指摘する人もいる。これは，ほかの言語に比べて文法上それほど複雑ではないので，英語は学びやすいに違いないと言いたいのだろう。
　このような主張は思い違いである。ラテン語は，文法的にはるかに複雑だと思える事実があるにもかかわらず，かつて主要な国際語だった。言語が国際語になるのは，その言語に備わっている構造的な特性によるのでもなければ，語彙の規模によるのでもなく，過去において偉大な文学の伝達手段であったからでもなく，それがかつて偉大な文化や宗教と関わりがあったからでもない。言語は古くから1つの主な理由，すなわちそれを話す人の影響力，とくに彼らの政治力，軍事力によって国際語になってきたのだ。

Point

原因・理由を表す接続詞
① because「〜なので」
I was absent from school **because** I had a headache.
（私は頭が痛かったので，学校を休んだ。）
② since「〜なので」
Since you look tired, you'd better take a rest.
（疲れているようなので，休んだほうがよい。）
③ as「〜なので」
As it was cold in the morning, I nearly caught a cold.
（朝寒かったので，かぜをひきそうになった。）

解説
　because は原因・理由を表す最も一般的な接続詞。because → since → as の順に原因・理由

を表す強さが弱くなる。

since は相手がすでに知っている原因・理由を述べる場合に使うことが多く，文頭に置くことが多い。

as は文頭に置くことがふつうである。

・**As** I can't swim, I don't want to go fishing.
（私は泳げないので，釣りには行きたくない。）

13 過度な健康志向が生む不健康(pp. 28〜29)

(1) ① ウ ② イ ③ ア ④ イ
(2) ウ，エ
(3) イ

解説

(1)① restrict「〜を制限する」 ② starved of 〜「〜が欠乏した」 ③ claim「〜と言い張る」 ④ due「〜することになっている」

(2)**ア** to eat foods that are essentially bad for them が誤り。食品が有害なのではなく，極端な食べ方のせいで不健康になっている。 **イ** due to viewing posts on Instagram が誤り。インスタグラムの投稿を見ること自体は問題ではない。 **ウ** 第2段落最終文(ll. 17-19)に一致。 **エ** 第2段落第4文(ll. 13-15)に一致。 **オ** has been reduced が誤り。オルトレキシアを患う人は増えている。

(3)**ア** 最終段落第2文(ll. 21-24)に不一致。 **イ** 最終段落第3文〜第4文(ll. 24-26)に一致。 **ウ** そのような記述はない。 **エ** そのような記述はない。

全文訳 ソーシャルメディアが，とある摂食障害をあおり立てている。その障害に陥ると「健康的」な食品を口にすることにこだわるあまり，かえって体調を崩してしまう。食事療法の専門家の話では，オルトレキシア，つまり患者が自分にとって「健康的」あるいは「正しい」と考える食品しか口にしない摂食障害は，インスタグラムのようなサイト上でクリーン・イーティングや健康であることがもてはやされるせいで，深刻な問題になりつつある。健康を絵に描いたような人になるのではなく，多くの人が食事を制限するあまり不健康になり，健康と成長に必要とされるきわめて重要な栄養物質が不足して，その結果，体重を減らし，虚弱になり，骨強度を低下させている。

オルトレキシアは，正式には承認されていないが，1977年にアメリカ人医師であり作家でもあるスティーブン・ブラットマンによって作られた用語だ。フィラデルフィア科学大学のクリスティーナ・ブレッシュによる調査が示すところでは，ほとんどの患者が，健康的な食事だけをとることに基礎をおいて理想化されたライフスタイルを披露するインスタグラムユーザーをフォローしている。「人は昔から健康的な食事をしようと努めてきました。それは新しいことでも何でもありません」とブレッシュ博士は話し

た。「ですが，私たちがいま目にしているのは，心身の健康に影響を及ぼすほどにまで人々がクリーン・イーティングを気にしているということであり，それはいままでに目にしたことはありません」彼女は，「健康志向」とソーシャルメディアによる情報伝達のスピードおよび届く範囲とが相俟って，オルトレキシアの発症に拍車がかかっているのだと話した。「信じられないくらい魅力的で幸せそうな人たちのソーシャルメディア上の画像を見ると，彼らはいわゆる〈健康的な〉食事で幸せになったと言い張るわけですから，こうした影響されやすい人たちもそのようなライフスタイルを認めることになります」

裏づけのデータが『精神疾患の診断・統計マニュアル』に提出される予定で，オルトレキシアの症例はいずれ公式に承認される。英国認定の食事療法専門家ルネ・マクレガーが言うには，この病気を特定する現行のプロセスは，しっかりとした根拠があるわけではなく，おおむね患者の食習慣が本人の健康にどれくらい影響を及ぼしているか，その程度に基づいている。「必ずしも体重や身体イメージと関連があるわけではありませんから，なかなか見分けがつきません」と彼女は話した。「心理的な衝動と言ったほうがよくて，食事を適切に制御できなくなるんです。ピザやケーキのようなものは，とにかく身体的に食べることができません。ますます多くの人が，自分は問題を抱えていると自覚する姿を目にしています。一般的に，こういった人たちは資格など有していないインスタグラマーをフォローしていて，このインスタグラマーがとても危険な食べ方を実際に言い広めています。ほとんど宗教のようなものです」

Point

関係代名詞の非制限用法

① I went to see my teacher, whom I found sick in bed.
（私は先生に会いに行ったが，その先生は病気で寝ていた。）
② We went to Rome, at which we parted.
（私たちはローマに行き，そこで別れた。）
③ She went to Paris, which is the capital of France.
（彼女はフランスの首都パリへ行った。）
④ Yesterday I met John, who is my cousin.
（私は昨日，いとこのジョンに会った。）

解説

「関係代名詞の非制限用法」はその前の先行詞の内容を補足的に説明する表現である。特に先行詞が固有名詞の場合は，すでに世界で1つのものだと限定されているので，非制限用法しか使えない。

14 モリー・ピッチャー　(pp. 30〜31)

(1)　主な活躍の舞台が戦場だった点(14字)
(2)　①イ　②ウ　③ア
(3)　全文訳 の下線部参照。
(4)　(A)F　(B)T　(C)T　(D)T　(E)F　(F)F

解説

(1)第1段落第6文(*ll.* 9-10)に However, these women's contributions were mostly away from the fighting. とある。「彼女は直接戦闘に参加した」のような答えも可。

(2)① obvious「明らかな」brave「勇敢な」oblivious「忘れっぽい」　② dimly「ぼんやりと」vaguely「漠然と」bitterly「苦々しく」　③ incredibly「信じられないほど，非常に」predictably「予想されるように」mildly「穏やかに」somewhat「多少，いくぶんか」

(3) Molly と a common nickname for Mary は同格関係にある。

(4)(A)「モリーはドイツで生まれた」ドイツ移民の子どもとして，ニュージャージーで生まれた。　(B)「モリーの夫は移民だった」アイルランドからの移民だった。　(C)「マーサ・ワシントンは"非戦闘従軍者"のリーダーだった」第3段落第1文(*ll.* 22-24)参照。　(D)「モリーが"モリー・ピッチャー"と呼ばれたのは，彼女がピッチャーを運んでいたからである」第3段落第4文〜最終文(*ll.* 26-30)参照。　(E)「モリーは，夫が戦死したため，彼の代わりを務めた」夫は暑さで卒倒したが，亡くなったわけではない。　(F)「ジョージ・ワシントンはモリーの勇気を，取るに足らないこととして無視した」非常に感銘を受けたので，彼女を名誉将校にした。

全文訳 19世紀初め，アメリカ人が，イギリスからの独立を求める戦いの歴史を書き始めたとき，彼らは祖国の精神を象徴するヒーローやヒロインを探した。国家のドラマの中で，主役を務められる男性は大勢いた。アメリカ合衆国の初代大統領を務めたジョージ・ワシントンは「建国の父」として当然選ばれた。しかし女性については，明確な主役がいなかった。ワシントンの妻のマーサ，星条旗を作った人物とされているベッツィー・ロス，愛国心の強いフィラデルフィアの主婦エスター・バート・リードなど，多くの女性たちがアメリカ独立のドラマで重要な役割を果たした。しかし，これらの女性たちの貢献は，ほとんど戦場から離れたものであった。歴史家たちが本当に探していたのは，戦場のヒロインだった。彼らは最終的に，かすかに覚えていたメアリー・ヘイズの物語に関心を向けた。兵士である夫の世話をするためワシントンの軍に従軍した，ペンシルベニアの女性だ。彼女はのちに，アメリカ独立戦争の伝説的ヒロイン「モリー・ピッチャー」として知られるようになった。

　メアリーは1744年，ドイツ系移民の子どもとして，ニュージャージー植民地で生まれた。そこで育てられた彼女は，16歳のとき，ペンシルベニアの町カーライルに引っ越して，アービンという名の医師の家で家事使用人の職に就いた。公的記録によれば，1769年，彼女はアイルランドからの移民で理髪師のウィリアム・ヘイズと結婚した。メアリーとウィリアムはカーライルでふつうの結婚生活を過ごしていたが，1777年，アービン医師がワシントンの軍の一部として独立戦争を戦うため，義勇兵の部隊を組織した。ウィリアムは，最初に入隊した兵士の1人となった。

　夫が軍に入隊したことで，メアリーは「非戦闘従軍者」になった。それは，マーサ・ワシントンによって率いられた兵士の妻たちの一団の1人で，パンなどを焼いたり，食事を配ったり，服や毛布を洗濯したり，病気や瀕死の兵士たちの世話をしたりした。キャンプでは，彼女はすぐに，モリーとして知られるようになったが，それはメアリーの一般的な愛称である。1778年の春に，ウィリアムは砲兵としての訓練を受けた。砲兵の仕事は，大砲に弾を込めて撃つことである。それからメアリーは「ウォーター・ガール」として働き始め，飲んだり，熱い大砲を冷やしたりするために水を必要とする砲兵に新鮮な水の入ったピッチャー，つまりバケツを運んだ。メアリー・ヘイズは結局，「モリー・ピッチャー」として知られるようになった。それは，戦場の兵士たちが水を必要としたとき，「モリー！　ピッチャー！」と声を上げる，その叫び声から来た。

　1778年6月28日，ニュージャージーの町モンマスコートハウスを占拠したイギリス軍に，ワシントンの軍が攻撃をかけた。メアリーはウォーター・ガールとして，夫の部隊と一緒にいた。その日の天候は，ものすごく暑かった。戦闘が続く中，暑さで疲れ切ったウィリアムは，自分の大砲の横で意識を失った。彼女の夫が戦場の外へ運び出されると，メアリーは彼に代わって，その日の終わりまで大砲に弾を込め，撃ち続けた。話によると，あるとき，イギリス側の弾丸が彼女のスカートのすそを引き裂いたという。彼女はそんなことは気にもせず，「これくらいで済んでよかったわ」と言って，大砲に弾を込め続けたと言われている。戦闘のあと，ワシントンはその勇気に大いに感銘を受け，メアリーを彼の軍の名誉将校にした。

Point

2語動詞

① They **looked for** heroes and heroines who symbolized the spirit of the nation.
（彼らは祖国の精神を象徴するヒーローやヒロインを探した。）

② Mary Hays followed Washington's army to **care for** her soldier husband.
（メアリー・ヘイズは，兵士である夫の世話をするため，ワシントンの軍について行った。）

③ She moved to the town to **take up** a position as a domestic servant.
（彼女は家事使用人の職に就くため，その町に引っ越した。）

解説

英語では，2つ以上の単語で1つの意味を表す**熟語**がよく使われる。その中で，look for 〜「〜を探す」，care for 〜「〜の世話をする」，take up「（仕事などに）就く」のように，単語2つで1つの動詞の働きをするものを2語動詞という。

「知っている単語しか使われていないのに，どうも文の意味がわからない」という場合，特別な意味を持つ2語動詞（そのほかの熟語）が使われていないかどうか，辞書で確認してみるとよい。

2語動詞は非常によく使われるので，少しずつ覚えていくように。今回の本文でも上記のほかに cool down「〜を冷ます」 call out「〜と大声で叫ぶ」などが使われている。

15 10代の母親たち　　　　(pp. 32〜33)

- (1) (A)ア　(B)イ　(C)イ
- (2) ①ウ　②ア
- (3) **全文訳** の下線部(a)，(b)参照。
- (4) イ，ウ

解説

(1)(A) attend「〜に出席する」 extend「〜を延ばす」 intend「〜をもくろむ」 pretend「〜のふりをする」
(B)離れていてややわかりにくいが，not only A but (also) B「A だけでなく B も」という形になっている。
(C) every two hours「2時間おきに」

(2)① demanding「要求の多い」 insistent「（要求などが）しつこい」 calm「静かな」 obedient「従順な」
② secure「安全な，安定した」 stable「安定した」 secular「世俗的な」

(3)(a) could は現在の事実に反する仮定を表す仮定法過去。some は「（中には）〜という人もいる」と解釈することもできるが，単に「何人かの」と取ることも可能→「何人かの10代の母親たちは，自分がもう一度子どもになれればいいのに，と思っている」
(b) That は「アメリカの15歳から19歳の少女1,000人当たりの出産数」を指す。「比率」と解釈すれば，「多い」の代わりに「高い」も可。A as well as B「B だけでなく A もまた」 developing ones = developing countries

(4)ア「コブナント・ハウスは，お金を儲けるために，多くの10代の母親たちの注意を引きつけようとしている」非営利組織なので，金儲けを目的とはしていない。　イ「デローレス・クレメンズには，5人も子どもがいる」as many as は「〜もの数の」の意味。第2段落参照。　ウ「コブナント・ハウスに来る前，ナターシャはホームレスだった」第4段落に「彼女は路上生活をしていた」とある。　エ「およそ350人の赤ちゃんが毎年コブナント・ハウスで生まれる」350人は，育児教室「マミー・アンド・ミー」を卒業する10代の母親たちの数。　オ「プラシダは，母親であることはとても楽しいと思っている」 very hard「とてもたいへん」と言っている。

全文訳 親は，子どもの最初の教師である。しかし，親の中には，よい手本から学ぶ機会のなかった人もいる。ニューヨーク市では，コブナント・ハウスという非営利組織が，ホームレスの若い母親がよい親になるための助けになろうとしている。

12人ほどの，シェルター（一時保護施設）に住む10代の母親が，週に4日，子育て教室に出席する。そのクラスの名前は，マミー・アンド・ミー（ママと私）だ。教師のデローレス・クレメンズは5人の子を持つ母親で，孫もいる。彼女は，赤ん坊をどのように入浴させるか，季節によってどのような服を着せるかというような，基本的な技

術を教えている。彼女は，自分の母親から，泣いている赤ん坊を抱き上げないように教えられた，1人の生徒のことを覚えている。その母親は，抱き上げたりすると，赤ん坊が愛情に飢え，あれこれしつこくねだる子どもになってしまうと言ったのだ。

クレメンズは言う。「私は言いました。『それは正しくない。赤ちゃんを抱いてあげなきゃ！ 理由があって泣いているの。抱っこしてあげないと，そのまま泣き続ける。抱っこして。抱き寄せて。抱きしめてあげて！』それから，彼女はそのようにし始めました。赤ちゃんはちょっと抱いてもらうこと，ちょっとした愛情がほしいだけなのです。それで，うまくいくのです！」彼女は，生徒たちはまた，母親から受けるような愛情を自分が受けることによって，自分たち自身がよい母親になる方法を学ぶのだと言う。クレメンズは，こう結ぶ。「私は，彼女たちが今までしてもらえなかったことを，彼女たちにしてあげているのです」

毎年，350人ほどの10代の母親が，コブナント・ハウスのマミー・アンド・ミー教室を卒業する。今日のクラスの出席者の中に，男の赤ちゃんと一緒に来たナターシャがいる。以前は，路上生活をしていた。彼女はコブナント・ハウスのシェルターの暖かさをありがたがっているだけでなく，レポーターのアダム・フィリップスに語ったように，より安定した生活を得ようとしている自分にコブナント・ハウスが行う援助についてもありがたいと思っている。ナターシャは言う。「履歴書やカバーレターの作成，就職の面接に必要なことすべてを手助けしてくれます。どんなことに興味があっても，仕事を見つける手伝いをしてくれます」

レポーター「高校には行きましたか」

ナターシャ「はい，行きました」

レポーター「卒業しましたか」

ナターシャ「いいえ，していません。最終学年のときに妊娠して，サボるようになって」

レポーター「そのことについて，自分の責任を受け入れようとしているようですね」

ナターシャ「そうです。そして，やり遂げたいと思っています」

(a)10代の母親の中には，自分自身がもう一度子どもになれたらいいのに，と思っている人もいる。18歳のプラシダには，その気持ちがわかる。彼女は，母親であることはたいへんだと言う。「真夜中に，2時間おきに起きないといけませんから。それに，外出して『自分のために，これを買おう』なんて言えません。だめです。おむつや，服，食べ物を買わないといけません。2人なんです。1人だけではないんです。だから，とてもたいへんです」

世界保健機関によれば，アメリカの15歳から19歳までの少女1,000人に対して41人の子どもが生まれている。(b)それは，ほかの先進諸国や，いくつかの発展途上国より多い。これに対し，北の隣人であるカナダの数値は14人である。

願望を表す仮定法過去

① Some teenage mothers **wish** they **could** be children themselves again.
（10代の母親の中には，自分自身がもう一度子どもになれたらいいのに，と思っている人もいる。）

② **If only** he **loved** me.
（彼が私を愛してくれさえすればいいのに。）

解説

〈S＋wish＋仮定法過去〉の文（S＝主語），〈If only＋仮定法過去〉の文で，「～だったらいいのに」という意味の，**現在の事実に反する願望**を表すことができる。

実現の可能性がまったくないか，非常に低い場合に用いられる。

16 マイケルのウサギ （pp. 34〜35）

(1) ①ウ ②イ ③ア ④ア ⑤イ
　　⑥ウ ⑦ウ
(2) エ
(3) 全文訳 の下線部(a), (b)参照。

解説

(1)① make excuses「言いわけをする」 ② become eager to *do*「しきりに〜したがる」 ③ neglect「〜を放置[無視]する」 ④ have words with 〜「〜と言い争う」 have a word with 〜は「〜とちょっと話をする」で，この話の内容に合わない。 ⑤ train O to *do*「O を〜するようにしつける」 ⑥ nuisance「じゃま者」 ⑦ get rid of 〜「〜を追い払う」

(2)マイケルの父親は「夕食にウサギを食べてしまおう」と言ったのだが，マイケルは「ウサギの1匹を夕食に招待しよう」と言ったと勘違いをした。

(3)(a) keep O company「O の相手をする」
　(b) What about *do*ing?「〜してはどうだろうか」 have O for dinner は「O を夕食として食べる」と「O を夕食に招待する」という2つの意味で使われている。父親の考えどおりに「ウサギの1匹を食べてはどうだろうか」とすると，あとのマイケルの反応につながらないので，have の訳し方を工夫して「ウサギを食べる」「ウサギを招待する」のどちらの意味にも取れるような日本語訳にできるとよい。

全文訳 　マイケルは6歳のときにウサギについてのテレビ番組を見て，ウサギを無性に飼いたくなった。毎日，彼は母親に「お母さん，ウサギを飼ってもいい？」と言い続けた。母親が言いわけをすると，「どうして飼ってはいけないの？」と言った。

　小さな子どもがペットを飼うとき，ほとんど世話をしなければならないのは親のほうだということを母親は知っていた。「あのね」と彼女は言った。「子どもは急に犬やウサギか何かを飼いたがって，動物がいなくては生きていけないと思ったり，動物をかわいがるし，世話をして，えさをちゃんとあげると思ったりする。けれど2, 3週間すると，テレビを見ることのような，ほかのおもしろいことを見つけて，ペットをほったらかしにするようになる。それから親とペットのことで言い争って，親は本来は子どもがしていなければならないことに，ますます多くの時間を費やさなければならなくなってしまうの。でも一方では，小さいときから子どもに動物をかわいがるようにしつけることはよいことよ」

　だから，とうとうマイケルの7歳の誕生日に，両親は1匹ではなく2匹のウサギを買ってあげた。

　父親はマイケルに「2匹飼うほうがいい。ウサギだけになったとき，(a)お互いの相手をするだろうからね」と言った。それから彼は妻に「両方オスか両方メスかを確かめただろうな。1年たって何百匹にもなると困るから」と言った。

　「だいじょうぶ。両方ともメスよ」とマイケルの母親は答えた。マイケルはウサギを飼って喜び，大きくなるにつれてますます大事にした。しかしすぐに，ウサギは両親にとってじゃま者になった。というのは，マイケルが学校に行っている間，彼らがウサギの世話をしなければならなかったからだ。

　彼らはウサギを追い払うさまざまな方法を考えようとした。そしてついに，マイケルの父親はひと思いにやるのがいちばんだと決意し，ある日，妻に言った。「(b)ウサギの1匹を今晩の夕食にどうだろう？」

　マイケルはうれしそうに笑い，母親が答える前に言った。「それはすばらしいよ，お父さん。でも，ウサギってスプーンを持つことができると思う？」

　彼らはまだウサギを2匹とも飼っている。

Point

〈使役動詞＋目的語＋原形不定詞〉の表現
① What **makes** *you* **think** so?
　（なぜあなたはそう思うのか。）
② Be sure to **let** *me* **know**.
　（必ず私に知らせてください。）
③ I **had** *my children* **clean** their rooms.
　（私は子どもたちに自分たちの部屋を掃除させた。）

解説
　「使役動詞」はそのあとに〈目的語＋原形不定詞〉を伴う。make，let のほかに have もこの意味で使われる。

17 絵をうまく描くには　　(pp. 36〜37)

(1)　ウ　　(2)　ア
(3)　Ⓐキ　Ⓑオ　　(4)　エ
(5)　ウ，エ

解説

(1) so obtained は後置修飾の句で，前の the two main branches にかかる。so は直前の文の「幹の部分を枝分かれさせた」という内容を指し，the two main branches so obtained で「そのようにして得られた[描かれた]2本の主な枝」という意味になる。

(2) suggest のあとに続く that 節内の動詞は〈(should ＋)動詞の原形〉を用いる。

(3) 下線部は at what is in front of them となる。what は関係代名詞。(look) at what is in front of them は「彼らの前にあるものを(見る)」の意味。

(4) この take は「〜を必要とする」の意味。

(5) ア looking at the big tree「大きな木を見ながら」，with two pencils「2本の鉛筆で」という記述は本文にない。　イ第1段落後半(*ll.* 9-11)に I don't know what to draw と I don't know how とある。　ウ第2段落第4文(*ll.* 13-15)に a rather ambitious work，第5文(*ll.* 15-16)に I never finished it. とあり，一致する。エ第2段落第7文(*ll.* 18-19)に一致。

全文訳　ある朝，私は1年生の教室で，小さな女の子たちを教えていた。そのうちのたいへん仲のよい2人が大きな紙と鉛筆を取り出し，席に着いて，絵を描く用意をした。しばらく考えてから，一方の子はたいへん大きな木を描き始めた。紙面のいちばん下から始めて，2本の線を引いた。その線はお互いに接近し，紙面の上のほうへ平行に進み，上端近くまで来ると再び広がり始めた。それから彼女は上端近くにあるこの幹の部分を枝分かれさせた。そのように描かれた2本の主な枝から，彼女は数本のもっと細い枝を描き，その枝を葉で覆い始めた。その間中ずっと，もう1人の小さな女の子はじっと見ていて，何もしなかった。しばらくして私は彼女に言った。「何を描くつもり？」早く描きなさいと促したわけではない。ただ知りたかったのだ。彼女は「何を描いていいかわからない」と言った。「別の木を描いたらどう？」と私は言った。彼女はまったく躊躇<ruby>躇<rt>ちゅうちょ</rt></ruby>することも恥ずかしがることもなく言った。「どう描いていいかわからない」

それは私には驚きであり，意外な発見であった。私はたくさんの絵を見るのが好きであるけれど，描き方についてはほとんど知らない。私自身の学校教育に美術はほとんどなかった。ある美術の授業と私が描こうとした1枚の絵——満月を背景にして枯れ木の大枝にとまっているフクロウ——を覚えているだけだが，私にしては，どちらかというと野心作であった。私はそれを仕上げなかった。経験が乏しいせいで，私は，画家は目の前にあるものをただ見て，描き写し，それを続けるうちに少しずつうまくなっていく

のだと単純に考えていた。だがごく最近になって，線を引き色を塗って，実物に近いものに見える像を描くことには，技術を要するのだとわかった。学び，練習し，身につけなければならないコツ，いやたくさんのコツがある。絵は実物のように見えると私たちは思っているが，実はそうではない。絵は平らだが，実物はそうではない。実物には奥行きがある。だから実物を平らな絵にするには，多くの技が必要で，そうしたコツを身につけなければならないのだ。

Point

〈with ＋目的語＋〜〉の表現

① **With** *his eyes* **fixed on her**, he began to tell.
　(視線を彼女に注いだまま，彼は語り始めた。)
② Don't speak **with** *your mouth* **full**.
　(口を食べ物でいっぱいにしたままで話をするな。)
③ He stood **with** *a pipe* **in his mouth**.
　(彼は口にパイプをくわえて立っていた。)
④ The dog ate **with** *his head* **nodding**.
　(犬は首を振り振り食べた。)

解説

〈with ＋目的語＋〜〉で使われている with は「付帯状況」を表す用法で，「〜したまま，〜しながら」と訳せばよい。目的語のあとにはいろいろな形の形容詞的なもの(現在分詞，過去分詞，形容詞，形容詞句や副詞句)がくる。

①の文では過去分詞，②の文では形容詞，③の文では副詞句，④の文では現在分詞が目的語のあとに続いている。

18 ビルで農業 (pp. 38〜39)

- (1) (A)**オ** (B)**ウ** (C)**エ** (D)**イ** (E)**ア**
- (2) ①**イ** ②**エ** ③**ウ** ④**ア**
- (3) 全文訳 の下線部参照。
- (4) **イ，ウ**

解説

(1)(A)場所を表す at「〜で」 (B) on *one's* knees「ひざまずいて」 (C) care for 〜「〜の世話をする」 (D) fade into 〜「(光などが)弱まって〜になる」 (E) in turn「次には」

(2)① share「〜を共用する，〜を共同で使う」 divide「〜を分割する」 co-own「〜を共同で所有する」 compete「争う」 ② a step in the right direction「正しい方向への第一歩」 right angle「正しい角度，直角」 right below「真下に」 ③ fed は feed「〜に肥料を与える」の過去分詞。 ④ back and forth「行ったり来たりして」 facade(＝façade)「建物の正面」 fringe「周辺部」

(3) If you walked 〜は，仮定法過去。not *A* but *B* は，「*A* でなく*B*」。

(4)**ア**「ケンジが使用しているエレベーターは，そのビルの屋上にある太陽電池によって稼働している」本文に太陽電池の話は出てこない。**イ**「著者の都市部の友達のほとんどは，植物を育てている」第2段落第6文(*ll.* 14-15)に In fact, most of my friends in the city grow tomato plants on windowsills or balconies. とある。most「ほとんどの」のような限定の強い単語があると正しくない文であることが多いが，この文は正しい。 **ウ**「ケンジの農園のおかげで，そのビルの住人による電気の使用が少なくなっている」第3段落第3文(*ll.* 19-21)と一致。 **エ**「サツマイモは，屋上農園で育てられると，より甘くなる」そのような記述はない。

全文訳

私は先日，ケンジという名前の農業従事者に会ったが，彼は，典型的な農夫ではない。ケンジは，東京の都心にあるオフィスビルで働いている。ほとんどの都市生活者と同様に，地下鉄で出勤し，エレベーターに乗って自分の職場に行く。しかし，同じエレベーターに乗っている，ほかの人たちとは違って，ケンジは，コンピュータのスクリーンの前で目をこらして1日を過ごしたりはしない。そうする代わりに彼は屋上に上り，1日中ひざをつき，愛情を込めて，地上50階にあるサツマイモ畑の面倒をみる。日が暮れると，服を着替え，エレベーターに乗って下に降り，大都市のまばゆい光と喧騒に戻っていく。

これは明らかに，私の祖父がしていた畑仕事とは違う。ケンジの仕事にも共通する部分はあるが，彼がいる場所とその決意から，農業を現代生活に持ち込もうという熱い思いがうかがえる。私の祖父の時代，子どもは都会でのよい仕事を求めて農家を去り，ほとんどの者が帰らなかった。

しかし最近は，食物を育てることが流行になってきている。畑に戻るのではなく，都会に畑の一部を持ってこようという思いが，確かに存在している。実際，都会に住む私の友人のほとんどが，窓台の上かバルコニーでトマトを育てている。今，「農夫」という言葉を聞くと，私は若くてクールで都会的なケンジ，指の爪の下に少しだけ土をつけた青年と，繁華街が目に浮かぶ。

流行であることに加えて，これらの屋上農園は，住人や環境にも恩恵がある。ケンジの屋上農園に広がるサツマイモは，食料を供給するほかに，その幅の広い葉が日陰を提供し，屋上をより低い温度に保つ。ビル内の人は，それほど頻繁にエアコンを使用しないため，必要なエネルギーも少なくなり，その結果，空調システムが排出する熱や汚染物質も少なくなる。双方に恩恵があるのだ。

植物はまた，交通や産業から排出される一酸化炭素を吸って，良質で，きれいな酸素に変える。この，シンプルだが洗練された，空気をきれいにするプロセスは，小さな一歩かもしれないが，正しい方向への第一歩だ。屋上農園がもっと一般的になれば，都会はたちまち，日々の都市生活の騒音や喧騒のはるか頭上で酸素を作り出す緑地によって覆われるかもしれない。

環境に恩恵をもたらすのに加えて，屋上農園は経済にも貢献する。植物は，肥料や水を与えられる必要があるし，雑草を抜いてくれる人も必要とするため，ケンジのような従業員が給料をもらって，ビルのオーナーが屋上に農園を造り，維持管理する手助けをし，何を植えたらよいのかについて助言もする。(サツマイモは，暑い太陽を好む一方，風に強いので好ましい。)

人材派遣会社パソナは農業が——都市部でもそれ以外でも——人気のある職業上の選択肢になることを望んでいる。パソナは，東京の都心の大手町地区にある自社のオフィスの地下で，農業研修プログラムを始めた。<u>もしあなたが，そのビルの正面入口から中に入ったとしても，若い人たちがそこの屋上でなく地下で，農業を学んでいるとは決して思わないだろう。</u>エレベーターに乗って2階下に行けば，バラが咲き，トマトの苗がワイヤーフレームを伝って上に伸び，レタスやカボチャが天井のライトに向かって葉を広げているのを見るであろう。別の部屋では，白衣を着た職員が部屋と部屋を行ったり来たりしながら，ボタンを押し環境を調整して作り出したそよ風に，イネが揺れている。

Point

to 不定詞

① The kids left the farm **to get** good jobs in the city.
（子どもたちは，都市でよい仕事を得るために農場を去った。）

② Plants need someone **to pull** weeds.
（植物には，雑草を抜く人が必要だ。）

③ Plants need **to be fed and watered**.
（植物は，肥料や水を与えられる必要がある。）

④ Kenji offers advice on **what to plant**.

（ケンジは，何を植えるかについてのアドバイスを提供する。）

解説

to 不定詞には**副詞的用法**（動詞などを修飾）・**形容詞的用法**（名詞を修飾）・**名詞的用法**（主語・目的語・補語になる）の3種類がある。

①は，副詞的用法。to get good jobs in the city が動詞 left を修飾している。

②は，形容詞的用法。to pull weeds が名詞（代名詞）someone を修飾。

③は，名詞的用法。to be fed and watered が動詞 need の目的語になっている。

・To be honest is the best policy.
（正直であることが，最もよい方針である。）
↑ to 不定詞が主語になる例

・What they need is to sleep.
（彼らに必要なのは，眠ることだ。）
↑ to 不定詞が補語になる例

このほかに，〈疑問詞＋to 不定詞〉で名詞の役割を果たす用法があり，この形で上記の名詞的用法と同様に，主語，目的語，補語になる。④では，what to plant が前置詞 on の目的語になっている。

19 言葉が生んだ誤解 (pp. 40〜41)

(1) (a)オ (b)エ (c)ウ (d)イ
(2) ①ウ ③イ
(3) 全文訳 の下線部②，④参照。
(4) 日本人ガイドは「ホテルのフロントデスク［受付］のところで」，アメリカ人観光客は「ホテルの建物の正面（玄関の前）で」と受け取った。

解説

(1)(a) insist on から考える。 (b) be full of 〜「〜でいっぱいである」 (c) in a loud voice「大きな声で」 (d) pay for 〜「〜の代金を支払う」 an extra hour は「余分にかかった1時間」。
(2)① take O aback「O をびっくりさせる」 ③「うそをついてそれから逃れる」
(3)② anxious to do「何としても［ぜひ］〜したいと思って」 soothe things over「（言い争いなどを）丸く収める」 ④ neither「両方とも〜ない」この場合は日本人ガイドとアメリカ人の両方。
(4)第4段落を参照。日本語でフロントと言えばホテルのフロントデスク［受付］を思い浮かべるが，英語の front は建物の正面（玄関）のこと。

全文訳 ある日本人観光ガイドが京都でアメリカ人夫妻を案内するよう頼まれた。彼は夫妻が泊まっているホテルのロビーから彼らの部屋に電話し，10分後に会うことにした。

1時間たったが，アメリカ人夫妻は現れなかった。ガイドがあきらめて立ち去ろうとしたちょうどそのとき，たいへん怒ったアメリカ人夫妻が通りからホテルに入ってきた。そこでそのガイドが，彼らが自分の客かどうかを尋ねると，その夫はかんかんになって，1時間遅れだぞとガイドを非難した。ガイドはびっくりして，自分は時間どおりに来て，約束の場所で待っていたと言ったが，そのせいでアメリカ人の夫はさらに怒ってしまった。この日本人はうそつきだ，自分と妻は1時間待っていた，この日本人が時間に遅れたのは間違いないと，そのアメリカ人の夫は大きな声で訴えた。（その日本人ガイドは約束の時間前からそこにいたので，）とうとう，明らかに真実でないことをそのアメリカ人が怒って主張するのに困りはてたが，②何としてもことを丸く収めたいと思って，ガイドは自分が悪かったと言って謝った。アメリカ人の夫はわめくのをやめたが，妻に言った。「ほら，こいつはうそをついていたのを認めたぞ！」日本人ガイドはがまん強くこれを聞き流し，事前の要望どおりにアメリカ人夫妻を案内した。彼らがホテルに戻って来たとき，ロビーはその夫妻の旅行団のほかのアメリカ人メンバーでいっぱいだった。夫は彼のガイドが1時間遅れてやって来て，うそをついて言い逃れようとしたいきさつを大きな声で，ほかのメンバーにすぐに言い始めた。このアメリカ人をなだめて，友好的な関係で別れようとする最後

の努力として，日本人ガイドは，クリスマスカードを送れるように，アメリカの住所を彼に尋ねた。自分が案内した外国人にいつもそうしていたからだ。

しかし，このことがそのアメリカ人をいっそう怒らせ，彼はほかのアメリカ人全員の前で，おまえは誠意のない友情を示してこびへつらい，1時間分の追加料金を払わせる気か，と大声で日本人ガイドを責め立てた。

数年後，その日本人ガイドは問題の根本は英語の使い方にあるのだと気づいた——彼が「フロントで」と言ったとき，和製英語で使われるように「ホテルのフロントデスクのところで」という意味だった。しかしそのアメリカ人は標準英語で使われるように「ホテルの建物の正面で」という意味にとった。だから，両者とも「時間どおり」に「正しい場所」にいた——④どちらもうそをついていなかったのだ。

アメリカ人の見解からすれば，日本人ガイドは自分が正しいと思うなら謝るべきではなかった。もし彼が言い返し，謝るのを拒んでいれば，最終的には（理想的には）事実が明らかになって，誤解が解けていただろうに。

Point

仮定法過去完了

① **If** I **had left** an hour earlier, I **could have met** him.

（私はもう1時間早く出発していれば，彼に会えただろうに。）

② I **wish** I **had studied** English harder in my youth.

（若い頃もっと一生懸命英語を勉強しておけばよかったのに。）

解説

仮定法過去完了は「**過去の事実に反する仮定および願望**」を表す表現であり，〈If＋主語＋had＋過去分詞～, 主語＋助動詞の過去形＋have＋過去分詞….〉で「もし（あのとき）～だったら，…だったのに」の意味を表す。
①の文は直説法の文に書き換えると次のようになる。
① ＝ I didn't leave an hour earlier, so I couldn't meet him.
（私はもう1時間早く出発しなかった，だから彼に会えなかった。）
②の文のように I wish の後に仮定法過去完了の形〈主語＋had＋過去分詞～〉が続くと，「（あのとき）～だったらよかったのに」と過去の事実に反する願望や後悔を表す。直説法で書き換えると，
② ＝ I am sorry I didn't study English harder in my youth.
（若い頃もっと一生懸命英語を勉強しなかったので残念だ。）

20 絶え間なく変化する社会秩序 (pp. 42～43)

(1) **イ**
(2) **A－エ　B－ア　C－エ**
(3) **イ**
(4) **ウ**

解説

(1)「『秩序』と言えば，安定や永続性という意味を含んでいた」第1段落の内容から考える。特に第5文～最終文 (*ll.* 5-9) に注目。
(2) A. be similar to ～「～に似ている，～とほぼ同じである」　B.「私たちが確実に言える唯一の特徴は，その絶え間ない変化だ」　C. at will「思いのままに」
(3) vow merely to *do*「～することだけを公約する」keep ～ as it is「～を現状のままに維持する」
(4) **ウ**「現代社会の重要な側面を特定するのはきわめて難しい。というのは，社会があまりに目まぐるしく変化するうえに，私たちが社会秩序を簡単に変えられると考える傾向にあるからだ」第3段落第1文～第3文 (*ll.* 18-21) に一致。

全文訳　過去2世紀の変革は急激かつ過激なあまり，社会秩序の最も本質的な特徴を変えてしまった。従来，社会秩序は揺るぎなく確固たるものだった。「秩序」と言えば，安定や永続性という意味を含んでいた。急速な社会変革は例外的なものであって，ほとんどの社会的変化は，小さな一歩が数多く積み重なって生じたものだ。人は，社会構造は柔軟性がなく，いつまでも変わらないものだと思いがちだった。家族や共同体が秩序の範囲内で懸命に自分の居場所を変えようとしたとしても，秩序の基本構造を変えられるという考えは無縁のものだった。人は現状を甘んじて受け入れる場合が多く，きっぱりと言ってのけた。「昔からこうだったし，これからもこうだ」

この2世紀の間，変化の速度が急速になるあまり，社会秩序は動的かつ柔軟な性質を帯びた。今や常に流動的な状態にある。近代の革命のことを話すとき，私たちは1789年（フランス革命）もしくは1917年（ロシア革命）を思い浮かべることが多い。しかし実を言うと，近頃は毎年が革命的だ。今日では，30歳の人でさえ不審がるティーンエージャーに嘘いつわりなく言うことができる。「私が若かった頃，世界は今とまるで違っていた」例えば，インターネットは1995年から2000年にかけて広く使われるようになったが，それはたった20年くらい前のことだ。今日，私たちはそれなしの世界を想像できない。

そういうわけで，現代社会の特徴をいくら定義しようと思っても，カメレオンの色を定義するのとほぼ同じだ。私たちが確実に言える唯一の特徴は，その絶え間ない変化だ。人はこのことに慣れ，私たちのほとんどが社会秩序を柔軟なもの，思いのままに作り出し改良できるものと考えている。昔の支配者の主な約束は，伝統的秩序を守ること，あるいは失われた黄金時代に立ち返ることでもあった。この

2 世紀の間，政治の原則は古い世界をぶち壊し，そこによりよい世界を築くのを約束することだった。最も保守的な政党でさえ，現状維持だけを公約にすることはない。だれもが社会改革，教育改革，経済改革を約束し——少なからずそうした約束を果たす。

　科学者が，地球の運動によって地震や火山噴火が生じることを予想するのと同じように，私たちは，過激な社会運動によって血で血を洗う暴力の暴発が生じると予想するかもしれない。19 世紀と 20 世紀の政治史はたびたび，恐るべき戦争と革命の連続だったと語られる。ここには真実も多いが，こうしたいやというほど知っている大惨事を挙げ連ねることは，いささか誤解を招くおそれがある。近代は，すさまじいレベルの暴力と恐怖だけでなく，平和と平穏も経験してきたのだ。

Point

名詞構文

① **Most social transformations** resulted from **the accumulation of numerous small steps**.

（ほとんどの社会的変化は，小さな一歩が数多く積み重なって生じた。）

② The Internet came into **wide usage** from 1995 to 2000.

（インターネットは 1995 年から 2000 年にかけて広く使われるようになった。）

解説

　名詞構文とは，his sudden death「彼の突然の死」や the beauty of the landscape「景色の美しさ」のように，動詞や形容詞の名詞形を使って〈主語＋動詞〉，〈主語＋ be 動詞＋形容詞〉などの関係を表した構文のことである。例文では，次のような関係が成り立っている。

① most social transformations ⇔ most societies transform(ed)

the accumulation of numerous small steps ⇔ numerous small steps accumulate(d)

② wide usage ⇔ is[was] widely used

動詞 transform，accumulate，use がそれぞれ名詞形の transformation，accumulation，usage を使って表されている。名詞構文を理解しておくと，わかりづらい文意の英文をきちんと解釈したり，日本語にしづらい英文をうまく和訳したりすることができる。

・動詞の名詞形を使った名詞構文

I informed him of **the safe arrival of the parcels**.

（荷物が無事に届いたと彼に知らせた。）

⇔ the parcels arrive(d) safely

I explained **my belief in his innocence**.

（私は彼の無実を信じていると説明した。）

⇔ I believe(d) that he is[was] innocent

・形容詞の名詞形を使った名詞構文

Emily is known for **her pride in her beauty**.

（エミリーは自分の美貌を鼻にかけていることで有名だ。）

⇔ she is proud of her beauty

Do not communicate **your absence from home** on social media.

（ソーシャルメディア上で，家を留守にすることを伝えてはいけない。）

⇔ you will be absent from home

21 生命と水　　　(pp. 44〜45)

> (1) **全文訳** の下線部(a)，(b)参照。
> (2) ②ウ　③ア
> (3) ① die, in または live[exist / survive], for
> 　　④ for survival[surviving / living] または
> 　　　to survive[live]
> 　　⑤ is used[useful]

解説

(1)(a) Without 〜, の部分に条件がある仮定法過去の表現。　(b) be in danger of 〜「〜という危機に瀕している」　make life impossible「生命活動を不可能にする（＝生きていけなくなる）」

(2)② livestock は「家畜」。　③少し構文がとりにくいが，How much of this is due to human activity「このうちのどれくらいが人間の活動によるものなのか」が主語であり，this は前文の内容の「降雨があてにできなくなり，砂漠が広がってきていること」を指す。

(3)①「水がなければ，人間はほんの数日で死ぬ[ほんの数日間しかもたない]。」　下線部は, but のあとに文頭の Humans can live for が省略されている。a matter of 〜「約[およそ]〜」　④「しかし，私たちは生き永らえるためだけに水を必要とするのではない。」　下線部の more than 〜は「〜にとどまらない」，a matter of survival は「死活[生きるか死ぬかの]問題」という意味。　⑤「産業界では，水は冷却液あるいは溶剤として使われている。」　下線部の serve は「（〜として）使える，（〜に）役立つ」という意味。

全文訳

水は地球の表面の約70%を占め，最もありふれた液体である。(a)水がなければ，地球上にはどんな生命も存在しないだろう。事実，生命の最も古い形態は海で生じ，数百万年を経て原始的な種が乾いた地上に姿を現し始めた。

人間やほかの動物は大部分が水分から成る体を持っており，食物から必要な液体を取り入れる少数の種は別として，健康のバランスを維持するために，定期的に水を飲まなければならない。人間は食物なしで数週間生きることができるが，水なしではほんの2，3日しか生きられない。

水は食物供給の面からも必要である。多くの人々は魚類を主な食物としているが，さらに重要なことに，すべての食物連鎖の基礎である植物は，発芽し，光合成を行い，成長するのに水を必要とする。

不幸なことに，世界の多くの地域で，水の供給が不足しており，うまく管理されていない。水不足は植物や家畜が成長できないということを意味する。人間は栄養失調になったり，直接的にはのどの渇きから，あるいは病気への抵抗力不足から死んでしまうかもしれない。近年，降雨がだんだんあてにできなくなってきたように思われ，砂漠が広がってきている。このうちのどれくらいが人間の活動によるものかは議論の余地があるとしても，ある程度は人間の活動のせいであるに違いない。かなりの降雨量があるイ

ギリスのような国でさえ，家庭，産業，農業が莫大な水を必要とするため，真水が不足することになるかもしれない。

人間や動物が成長するには，十分な水だけでなく，きれいな水も必要である。多くの生物が水中に生息しているが，その中にはコレラ菌のような人間の生命に有害な生物も含まれる。飲料水には，有毒なミネラルや化学汚染物質が含まれていないことも必要なのである。

しかし，水は単に生きるか死ぬかという問題にとどまるものではない。私たちは自分自身や自分の持ち物を清潔にしておくのに水が必要だし，輸送手段として，工場や水力発電所の動力源として水を使っている。また産業界では水は冷却液や溶剤として役に立っている。水から重要な無機物を抽出することもできる。また水を眺め，水の音を聞くだけで，精神的に生き返ることもしばしばある。水は多くの宗教で重要な象徴であり，しばしば儀式で大きな意味を持つほど，私たちの生活の中で欠くことのできない部分を占めている。

悲しいことに，私たちは水を世界のごみ箱——人間の排泄物から放射性物質に至るまで，あらゆる種類の廃棄物の便利なごみ捨て場としても扱っている。ほかの多くの汚染物質が知らないうちに川や湖や海に行きついている。(b)私たちは，水中に生息する非常に多くのさまざまな種が生きていけなくなり，自分たちの命そのものが依存している水の供給を汚染するという危機に瀕している。

Point

if を使わない仮定法

① **Were I** as rich as she, I *would* travel all over the world.
　（彼女くらい金持ちだったら，ぼくは世界中を旅するだろうに。）

② **Without** water, there *would* be no life.
　（水がなければ，生物は存在しないだろう。）

③ You **couldn't** do that!
　（そんなのできっこないさ！）

解説

① **if の省略**：条件節の if が省略されると，倒置が起きて〈were[had，should など]＋主語〉の語順になる。

② **if 節の代用**：不定詞，分詞構文，副詞（句），主語の名詞などに条件の意味が含まれると，仮定法が用いられる場合がある。

③ **条件節の省略**：「ひょっとしたら」「しようと思えば」などを表す条件節が省略されて，帰結節だけが残る場合がある。

①の場合は，倒置した語順から仮定法とわかる。②③の場合は，一般に助動詞の過去形があれば，仮定法であると考えてよい。

22 手抜きする人を減らすには (pp. 46～47)

(1) (a)ア (b)ウ (c)イ (d)ウ
(2) 全文訳 の下線部参照。
(3) イ，エ，オ，キ

解説

(1)(a) integrate「～を統合［結集］する」（＝ combine「～を結合する」） (b) decline「低下する」（＝ diminish「減少する」） (c) detect「～がわかる，～を確かめる」（＝ perceive「～を知る，～がわかる」） (d) calculate「～を計算［計測］する」（＝ measure「～を測る」）
(2) social laziness develops は直訳すると「社会的手抜き［怠慢］が生じる」だが，文脈から「集団の中で怠ける」と解釈する。there is no way for people to tell ～ の for people は to 不定詞の意味上の主語。「人が～を判断する方法はない」how well they are doing「自分がどのくらいよく働いているか」→「自分の仕事ぶり」とする。
(3)ア第1段落の内容と不一致。 イ第2段落第1文 (*ll.* 8-9) と一致。 ウそのような記述はない。 エ第2段落第2文～第4文 (*ll.* 9-14) と一致。 オ第3段落第3文～第5文 (*ll.* 21-25) と一致。 カそのような記述はない。 キ最終段落の内容と一致。

全文訳 集団のメンバーが協力して働くと，一個人でできることよりも明らかに多くのことを達成できる。実際，人間の功績の中には，数人が関与して，それぞれの貢献を結集するグループプロセス（集団過程）を通してしか成し得ないものがある。経済的，技術的，政治的に複雑な現代社会は，だれひとりそのすべてを習得しようとは決して思わないほどの多様な技能を要求する。産業，科学，政府関連のほとんどの事業には今や，異なる分野の専門知識を提供する多くの専門家が必要になる。

しかし，グループプロセスを研究している研究者は，集団の規模が増すにつれ，メンバーひとりひとりの貢献が低下する傾向にあることを発見した。1920年代の後半，研究者は，人がみんなで協力してロープを引っぱるとき，自分ひとりで引っぱるときより力を入れないことをつきとめた。ひとりで引っぱるときは約63 kg の力で引っぱるのに，2人の人間が一緒に引っぱると，力は126 kg（2 × 63）ではなく118 kg になった。3人では160 kg の力で引っぱり，これはひとりで引くときの約2.5倍にすぎない。この研究やそのほかの研究から，人は集団の一員になると，ひとりのときより熱心には働かなくなるという結論が導かれた。どうやら，共通の仕事に多くの貢献者がいると，個々人は手を抜くらしい。つまり，怠けるのだ。

社会的インパクト理論では，集団が大きくなるほど，メンバーひとりにかかる成果に対する圧力は小さくなる，と考える。この理論の指摘によれば，集団の仕事に対する責任が分散されることで，個々人は力を尽くさなくなる。社会心理学者スティーブン・ハーキンズは1980年代後半に，

厳密に言えば，仕事の匿名性こそが手抜きを助長するのだと指摘した。自分がどれくらい貢献しているのかだれにも確かめようがないと個々人が考えていると，全員が生産を減らす傾向にある。実験者が個々人の貢献度を計測するときのように，個々の貢献が特定され得るときは，手抜きが減る。

研究者は，他者に評価されることが人を働かせ続ける唯一の要点ではないことを発見した。同じ仕事をして，ほかのだれかの以前の仕事ぶりと比較することで自分自身の仕事ぶりを評価できるとき，人は熱心に働く。たとえ実験者がその貢献度を算出できなくても。自己評価はどうやら，職務の「標準的な」遂行力に劣っていないとか，それよりも優れているといった満足感をもたらすらしい。人は自分の仕事ぶりを判断する方法がないとき，集団の中で怠けるようだ。

Point

従属接続詞 as「～するにつれて」
As groups increase in size, each group member's contribution tends to decline.
（集団の規模が増すにつれ，メンバーひとりひとりの貢献度は減少する傾向にある。）
解説
接続詞 as は「～するにつれて，～するにしたがって」のように「比例」の意味を表す。この意味では比較級を伴うことが多い。
・As he grew up, he became stronger and stronger.
（彼は成長するにつれて，ますます強くなった。）
・As I climbed the mountain, it became colder.
（山を登るにつれ，寒くなった。）

23 外国語の習得　　　(pp. 48〜49)

(1)　**ウ**
(2)　① foreign language instruction
　　②(young) children
　　③ foreign language study
(3)　**イ**
(4)　アメリカ(の学校のこと)。第3段落の3
　　番目のセンテンス。
(5)　the teaching of foreign languages
(6)　**全文訳** の下線部参照。

解説

(1)最初の文にある Foreign language instruction should come early in the educational process で明らかである。
(2)①第 1 段落第 2 文以降(*ll*. 2-8) の it はすべて foreign language instruction「外国語教育」を指す。
　②「子どもたち」を指す。　③直前の文の主語を指す。
(3)第 1 段落第 1 文(*ll*. 1-2) に，early in the educational process, basically at the elementary level とあるので，小学生の年齢を考えればよい。
(4)第 3 段落第 3 文(*ll*. 19-20) の for Americans に注目。アメリカ人に向けて書かれた文章であることから推測する。
(5)主節と副詞節の主語が同じだから if 節内の〈主語＋be 動詞〉が省略されている。
(6) already established in their minds が前の名詞 the patterns(of language) を修飾している。

全文訳

外国語教育は教育課程の早いうちに，基本的には初等教育の段階で行うべきである。その理由は，外国語教育は子どもが世の中を認識する力を根本的に形づくるのに役に立つからである。外国語教育は子どもに，世の中には自分の周りで見るものとたいへん違い，自分自身を順応するようにしなければならないものがたくさんあるという事実を受け入れさせる助けとなりうる。幼い子どもは簡単に楽しみながら外国語を学習するということからも，外国語教育は早いうちに行われるべきである。その段階では外国語教育は教育の本当におもしろい要素の 1 つになるはずで，学校教育の遅い時期に外国語教育を受けた何世代もの生徒に思われていたような無意味な骨折り仕事ではないのである。

母国語を話す人や AV 教材による語学授業といった現代的で，より効率的な技法も幼い子どもには特に効果がある。その段階では，子どもが自分の母国語でそうしたのと同じように，模倣と反復によって外国語を学習するのが彼らにとって自然なことである。子どもが大きくなればなるほど，ますますこの方法に抵抗するようになり，要素ごとに外国語を(d)彼らの頭にすでにある言語様式に置き換えるという合理的努力に頼り，その過程で話し手というよりはむしろ文法家になるのである。

どの言語を勉強すべきかという問題は，それらをいつ勉強すべきかということほど重要ではないであろう。外国語を選ぶ 1 つの基準は後の人生で予見できる実用性であろう。このような観点から言えば，スペイン語，フランス語，ドイツ語，イタリア語がアメリカ人にとってのふつうの好みだろう。もう 1 つの基準は英語とどれほど違う言語であるかということだろう。その違いが大きければ大きいほど，世界の多様性を理解したり，どの言語にもある論理的な限界を認識する点でも，その経験から得られる価値はますます大きくなるだろう。現実的な有用性とお互いに異なる要素をあわせ持つ言語を選び出すとすれば，日本語，中国語，アラビア語，ヒンズー語，スワヒリ語，ロシア語のような，重要だが英語とはたいへん異なる言語となるであろう。

外国語学習には現在不評の理由があることは私にはわかっている。外国語学習は大部分の若者には刺激のない，ほとんど関連のないことの丸暗記の作業だと考えられている。これらの批判は，今日，私たちの学校で行われている多くの外国語教育の概念とその実践を考えたとき，かなりの妥当性がある。しかし外国語の授業がうまく理解され，行われれば，次世代の人々に将来の国際社会の一員として成功するための準備をさせるという点で大切な要素となるだろう。

Point

比較表現

① **The older** she grew, **the more attractive** she became.
(彼女は年齢を重ねれば重ねるほど，魅力的になった。)
② Silver is **less valuable than** gold.
(銀は金ほど価値がない。)

解説

①〈the ＋比較級, the ＋比較級〉で「〜すればするほどますます…」という意味で，比較級を用いた重要表現のひとつ。このほかに以下のようなものがある。
・〈比較級＋ and ＋比較級〉:「ますます〜」
It is getting **warmer and warmer**.
(だんだん暖かくなってきた。)
・〈all the ＋比較級＋ because[for] 〜〉:「〜なのでいっそう…」
I like Ian **all the better for** his shyness.
(イアンには内気なところがあるから，私はなおさら彼が好きだ。)
②〈less ＋原級＋ than ...〉で「…ほど〜ではない」という意味で，not as[so] 〜 as ... を用いて書き換えることができる。
②＝ Silver is **not as[so]** valuable **as** gold.

24 テクノロジーの進歩とその制御（pp. 50〜51）

(1) **全文訳** の下線部参照。
(2) **ウ**
(3) **ウカ**
(4) **イ**
(5) A. 人類の繁栄を促進する技術の進歩
　　 B. 人としての尊厳および幸福に脅威をもたらす技術の進歩

解説

(1) not one of 〜「〜のひとりも…ない」（= none of 〜）
fail to *do*「〜できない，〜し損なう」 意味上は「〜できない者はひとりもいない」という二重否定になることに注意。

(2) 下線部の直後に individuals could not freely develop nuclear technology on their own or traffic in the parts necessary to create atomic bombs とある。on *one's* own「勝手に，独断で」　**イ**は，規制対象として「個人」に言及していないため，不適切。

(3) these extremes は「こうした両極端」という意味。第1段落で，規制対象になっている技術の例として「核兵器」が挙げられている一方，第2段落では，規制対象になっていない技術として「情報技術（IT）」が例として挙げられていることから考える。

(4) stand in the way of 〜「〜の邪魔[妨げ]になる」＝ interrupt 〜　**ア** facilitate は「〜を促進する」という意味の動詞。

(5) 第4段落第1文の後半(*ll.* 32-33)にある discriminate between those technological advances that promote human flourishing, and those that pose a threat to human dignity and well-being に着目する。

全文訳　新しい技術には，最初から恐ろしいために，その発達と使用に対して政治的規制を確立する必要性がすぐさま合意形成されるものがある。1945年の夏，史上初の原子爆弾がニューメキシコ州アラモゴードで爆発したとき，その事態を目のあたりにしただれひとりとして，恐ろしいほどの新たな破壊力が生まれたことを理解できない者はいなかった。こうして，核兵器はその出発点から政治的規制で包囲された。個人は独自で核技術を思うままに開発したり，原子爆弾の製造に必要な部品を不正に売買したりすることができなくなり，やがて，1968年の核不拡散条約に署名した国々は核技術の国際取引を規制することに同意した。

ほかの新技術の中には，はるかに害がないように見えて，それだけに規制がほとんどないか，まったくないものがある。パソコンやインターネットがその例だ。こうした新しい形の情報技術（IT）は富を生み出し，情報へのアクセスを，ひいては政治的権力をより民主的に広め，ユーザー間にコミュニティを創り出すことを約束した。人は情報革命の悪影響を必死になって探さなければならなかった。これまでに見つけた問題は，いわゆる情報格差（つまり，IT利用についての不均衡）やプライバシーへの脅威といった問題だが，そのどちらも正義や道徳に関するきわめて重大な問題とは言えない。政治的な権力や影響力が強い社会の中には，IT利用を規制しようとする試みがまま見られるものの，近年は，国内レベルでも国際レベルでも，ITは最低限の規制管理だけで発展してきた。

バイオテクノロジーはこうした両極端のほぼ中間に属する。遺伝子組み換え作物やヒト遺伝子工学は，パソコンやインターネットよりもはるかに人を不安にさせる。しかし，バイオテクノロジーは同時に，人の健康や幸福に重要な恩恵を約束する。嚢胞性線維症（のうほうせいせんい）や糖尿病の子どもを治療できるような先端技術を見せられると，人はその技術に対する不安が進歩の妨げになる理由をはっきりと口にするのが難しいことに気づく。新しいバイオテクノロジーに異を唱えるのは，その開発が臨床試験での失敗をもたらしたり，遺伝子組み換え食品に対する致命的なアレルギー反応をもたらしたりすれば，最も簡単なことだ。しかし，バイオテクノロジーの現実的な脅威は，はるかに微妙なものであり，したがって実際的な意味で天秤にかけるのは難しいのだ。

このような技術から生じる課題に直面する際，善と悪が密接に関連していて，考えうる対応策はひとつしかないように私には思える。各国が技術開発とその使用を政治的に規制し，人類の繁栄を促進する技術の進歩と，人としての尊厳および幸福に脅威をもたらす技術の進歩とを見分ける機関を設立することだ。こうした規制機関がまずは，国内レベルでこの区別を徹底させる権限を与えられ，最終的にはその範囲を国際レベルにまで拡大させなければならない。

Point

否定語句を使わない否定表現

① I **failed to** persuade her.
（私は彼女を説得することができなかった。）
② Jack is **anything but** a hero.
（ジャックは決して英雄ではない。）
③ She is **far from** (being) a fool.
（彼女は決してばかではない。）

解説

否定語句がないため，一見すると否定文には見えないが，意味上は否定文になる慣用表現。① fail to *do*「〜し損ねる」→「〜することができない」② anything but 〜「〜以外の何か」→「決して〜ではない」　③ far from 〜「〜には程遠い」→「決して〜ではない」　ほかにもさまざまな否定表現があるので，いくつか例を挙げておく。

・He is **free from** bias.
（彼は偏見にとらわれない。）
・This view **remains[has yet] to** be proved.
（この説はまだ証明されていない。）
・I **know better than to** quarrel with her.
（私は彼女とけんかするほどばかではない。）
・It is beautiful **beyond** description.
（それは言葉で言い表せないほど美しい。）

25 ホテルでの仕事　　（pp. 52〜55）

> (1)　**全文訳** の下線部(a), (b)参照。
> (2)　①**イ**　②**イ**　③**エ**　④**ア**　⑤**ウ**
> (3)　**ウ, オ**

解説

(1)(a) should「〜すべきだ」，be paid は「給料を支払われる」の意。should not have to *do*「〜する必要などないはずだ」　(b) them は doilies を指す。

(2)①「ただちに」　②I did it の前に書かれている内容から判断できる。　③take the risk of *do*ing「〜する危険を冒す」　④**ア** impatience「いらいらした気持ち」　⑤what it looked like のあとに the real world が省略されていて，「現実の世界のように見えるもの」の意味。直前の the real world「現実の世界」と対比している。

(3)**ア**「おじのホテル」ではなく，「おばのホテル」で働いていた。　**イ**第1段落最終文（*ll.* 5-6）と異なる。**ウ**第2段落第1文〜第2文（*ll.* 7-9）と一致。　**エ**第3段落参照。チップに対しての不満を言ったのではなく，給料を高くしてくれたらチップをもらわなくてもすむと言った。　**オ**第6段落の内容と一致。**カ**配膳室係(はいぜん)が自分の話をしたのではない。

全文訳

　ある夏，おばの経営するホテルで働いたとき，私は17歳や18歳であったに違いない。私はどれくらいのお金をもらったかわからないが，1か月に22ドルだったと思う。私は応接係や食堂給仕人の助手として，11時間労働と13時間労働とを交互に繰り返した。午後に応接係をしているときにはD夫人——チップを1度もくれたことのない病弱な女性——にミルクを運ばなければならなかった。世の中とはそんなものだった。毎日長い時間働いてもそれに対して何ももらえなかった。

　ここはニューヨーク市郊外の海辺のリゾートホテルだった。夫たちは市内へ働きに行き，妻たちはそこに残ってトランプをするのだった。だからいつもブリッジ用のテーブルを出さなければならなかった。それから夜には男たちがポーカーをするのだった。だから彼らのためにテーブルの用意をし，灰皿などをきれいにするのだった。私はいつも夜遅く，2時ぐらいまで起きていた。だから実際のところ，1日に13時間あるいは11時間働いたのだった。

　チップの習慣のように，私が好きでないものがあった。(a)私たちはもっと給料を支払われるべきだし，そうすればチップをもらう必要などないはずだと思った。しかし私が経営者のおばにそのことを申し出たとき，私はただ笑われただけであった。彼女はみんなに言った。「リチャードはチップがほしくないんだってさ。ヒーヒー。チップがほしくないんだって。はっはっはっ」世の中は何もわかっていないこの種のまぬけなうぬぼれ屋でいっぱいなのだ。

　ところで，一時期，市内の仕事から帰って来たとき，すぐに飲み物に氷を入れてほしいという男たちがいた。さて私と一緒に働いているもう1人の男は，私より前から応接係をしていた。彼は私より年上で，ずっとこの仕事に詳しかった。あるとき彼は私に次のように言った。「おい，ちょっと。いつもあのアンガーというやつに氷を持って行くんだが，彼はチップをくれたことがない。10セントさえもね。今度，氷を彼らが頼んでも，言うことを聞くなよ。そうすりゃ，あいつらはお前をもう1度呼ぶだろうよ。あいつらがお前をもう1度呼んだら，『あっ，すみません。忘れていました。ときどき忘れるんですよ』と言ってやりな」

　そのとおりにやってみた。するとアンガーは私に15セントもくれたのだ！　しかし今，私がそのことを振り返ってみると，私より仕事に詳しいもう1人のその応接係は，実際のところ何をしたらよいのかを知っていて，もう1人のやつ（私）が困ったことにぶつかる危険に直面するように，わざと言ったのだ。彼は，このアンガーというやつがチップをくれるよう仕込む仕事を私にさせたのだ。彼はそんなことは何も言わなかったが，彼は私にそんなことをさせたのだ。

　私は食堂給仕人の助手として，食堂のテーブルを片づけなければならなかった。テーブルからそばの盆に皿を積み上げる。そして皿がかなり高くなると，それを台所へ運ぶ。そして新しい盆を取る。2段階でこれをすべきなんだがすなわち古い盆を持ち去って，新しいのを手元に置く——しかし私は「1度にそれをやってみよう」と考えた。だから私は新しい盆を下にすべり込ませ，古い盆を同時に引き抜こうとしたところ，すべり落ちた——ガチャン！　ひとつ残らず床にぶちまけたのだ。言うまでもなく，すぐさま問いつめられた。「お前は何をしていたんだ。皿はどうして落ちたんだ」私が盆を取り扱う新しい方法を発明しようとしていたと，どうして説明することができようか。

　デザートの中に，小さな皿の上に敷物を敷いて，たいへんきれいにして出されてくるコーヒーケーキのようなものがあった。しかし，台所の奥に行けば，配膳室係と呼ばれている人がいるのだった。彼が困っていたのは，デザートのための敷物を用意することだった。この男は炭鉱労働者か何かだったに違いない。たいへん短く丸々とした太い指をして，がっちりとした体格だった。彼は敷物の束を手に取るわけだが，敷物はプレス加工か何かで製造されていて，1枚残らずぴったりくっついているものだから，(b)こんな(短くて太い)指で，皿の上に敷物を敷くために，彼はそれらを1枚ずつ取ろうとするのだった。私は，彼がこれをしているとき「この敷物め！」と彼が言うのをいつも聞いていた。そして私は「何という好対照なんだろう——テーブルについている人は敷物が敷かれた皿の上のこのおいしいケーキを食べる。一方，短く太い親指をしたその台所の奥の配膳室係は『この敷物め！』と言っている」と考えたことを覚えている。だからそのような違いが，現実の世界と現実のように見えるものの間にあった。

助動詞

① She **must have** been very pretty in her youth.

（彼女は若い頃，たいへんかわいらしかったに違いない。）

② She **must be** a high school student.

（彼女は高校生に違いない。）

③ When he was a child, he **would** get up early.

（彼は子どもの頃，早起きしたものだ。）

④ She **needn't** have been anxious.

（彼女は心配するには及ばなかったのに。）

解説

　ここでは①②の must，③の would，④の need について説明する。

　must には「**～しなければならない**」のほかに「**～に違いない**」という意味がある。

・He **must**（＝ has to）work hard.

（彼は一生懸命勉強しなければならない。）

・She **must** be rich.

（彼女は金持ちに違いない。）

　③の **would** は「**～したものだ**」という意味の過去の習慣を表している。

　④の **needn't** は「**～するに及ばない**」という助動詞で，そのあとに〈have ＋過去分詞〉が続くと「～するに及ばなかったのに」となる。